The Economic Value of Water Quality

NEW HORIZONS IN ENVIRONMENTAL ECONOMICS

General Editors: Wallace E. Oates, *Professor of Economics, University of Maryland, USA* and Henk Folmer, *Professor of General Economics, Wageningen University and Professor of Environmental Economics, Tilburg University, The Netherlands*

This important series is designed to make a significant contribution to the development of the principles and practices of environmental economics. It includes both theoretical and empirical work. International in scope, it addresses issues of current and future concern in both East and West and in developed and developing countries.

The main purpose of the series is to create a forum for the publication of high quality work and to show how economic analysis can make a contribution to understanding and resolving the environmental problems confronting the world in the twenty-first century.

Recent titles in the series include:

Sustainable Small-scale Forestry
Socio-economic Analysis and Policy
Edited by S.R. Harrison, J.L. Herbohn and K.F. Herbohn

Environmental Economics and Public Policy
Selected Papers of Robert N. Stavins, 1988-1999
Robert N. Stavins

International Environmental Externalities and the Double Dividend
Sebastian Killinger

Global Emissions Trading
Key Issues for Industrialized Countries
Edited by Suzi Kerr

The Choice Modelling Approach to Environmental Valuation
Edited by Jeff Bennett and Russell Blamey

Uncertainty and the Environment
Implications for Decision Making and Environmental Policy
Richard A. Young

Global Warming and the American Economy
A Regional Assessment of Climate Change Impacts
Edited by Robert Mendelsohn

The International Yearbook of Environmental and Resource Economics
2001/2002
A Survey of Current Issues
Edited by Henk Folmer and Tom Tietenberg

Sustainable Farm Forestry in the Tropics
Social and Economic Analysis and Policy
Edited by S.R. Harrison and J.L. Herbohn

The Economic Value of Water Quality
Edited by John C. Bergstrom, Kevin J. Boyle and Gregory L. Poe

Implementing European Environmental Policy
The Impacts of Directives in the Member States
Edited by Matthieu Glachant

The Economic Value of Water Quality

Edited by

John C. Bergstrom

University of Georgia

Kevin J. Boyle

University of Maine

Gregory L. Poe

Cornell University, USA and the Jackson Environmental Institute (JEI/Centre for Social and Economic Research on the Global Environment (CSERGE), University of East Anglia, UK

NEW HORIZONS IN ENVIRONMENTAL ECONOMICS

Edward Elgar
Cheltenham, UK • Northampton, MA, USA

Published by
Edward Elgar Publishing Limited
Glensanda House
Montpellier Parade
Cheltenham
Glos GL50 1UA
UK

Edward Elgar Publishing, Inc.
136 West Street
Suite 202
Northampton
Massachusetts 01060
USA

A catalogue record for this book
is available from the British Library

Library of Congress Cataloguing in Publication Data

The economic value of water quality/edited by John C. Bergstrom, Kevin J. Boyle, and Gregory L. Poe.
        p.cm.—(New horizons in evironmental economics)
   Includes bibliographical references and index.
   1. Water-supply—Economic aspects—United States. 2. Drinking water—Economic aspects—United States. 3. Water quality management—United States. I. Bergstrom, John C. (John Clark) II. Boyle, Kevin J. III. Poe, Gregory L. IV. Series.

   HD1694.A5 E262001
   333.91—dc21

2001023726

ISBN 1-84064-047-2

Printed and bound in Great Britain by Bookcraft (Bath) Ltd.

Contents

List of Figures   *vii*
List of Tables   *ix*
List of Contributors   *xii*
Preface   *xiv*

1. Economic Value of Water Quality: Introduction and Conceptual
   Background   1
   John C. Bergstrom, Kevin J. Boyle and Gregory L. Poe

2. Determinants of Ground Water Quality Values: Georgia and
   Maine Case Studies   18
   John C. Bergstrom, Kevin J. Boyle and Mitsuyasu Yabe

3. Information and the Valuation of Nitrates in Ground Water,
   Portage County, Wisconsin   38
   Gregory L. Poe and Richard C. Bishop

4. Measuring the Value of Protecting Ground Water Quality from
   Nitrate Contamination in Southeastern Pennsylvania   66
   Donald J. Epp and Willard Delavan

5. Ground Water, Surface Water, and Wetlands Valuation in Ohio   83
   Alan Randall, Damitha DeZoysa and Side Yu

6. Assessing the Accuracy of Benefits Transfers: Evidence From
   a Multi-Site Contingent Valuation Study of Ground Water Quality   100
   Timothy P. VandenBerg, Gregory L. Poe and John R. Powell

7. Benefits Transfer: The Case of Nitrate Contamination in
   Pennsylvania, Georgia and Maine   121
   Willard Delavan and Donald J. Epp

8. A Preliminary Meta Analysis of Contingent Values for Ground
   Water Quality Revisited   137
   Gregory L. Poe, Kevin J. Boyle and John C. Bergstrom

9. Summary and Conclusions   163
   Kevin J. Boyle, John C. Bergstrom and Gregory L. Poe

Index   169

List of Figures

Figure 1.1 Water quality valuation process   4

Figure 3.1 Example of general information provided in stage 1
            with info questionnaires, Wisconsin case study   42

Figure 3.2. Stage 1 and stage 2 distributions of expectations that
            Nitrate levels will exceed government standards in
            the next five years, Wisconsin case study   49

Figure 3.3 WTP as a function of nitrate levels: subjective
            probability and nitrate exposure models, Wisconsin
            case study   62

Figure 4.1 Information quiz, Pennsylvania case study   69

Figure 5.1 Ground water, surface water and wetlands protection
            programs, Ohio case study   85

Figure 5.2 Sampling Design for Ohio case study   86

Figure 5.3 Density function, estimated WTP (zeros real, gamma),
            Ohio case study   96

List of Tables

Table 2.1.   Mean values for explanatory variables used in option
              price equations for ground water protection in Georgia
              and Maine case studies   25

Table 2.2a.   Ad hoc option price equation results for ground
              water protection, Georgia case study   26

Table 2.2b.   Ad hoc option price equation results for ground
              water protection, Maine case study   28

Table 2.2c.   Ad hoc option price equation (without CONCERN
              variable) results for ground water protection, Georgia
              case study   30

Table 2.2d.   Ad hoc option price equation (without concern
              variable) results for ground water protection,
              Maine case study   32

Table 2.3.   Utility theoretic option price equation results for
              Ground water protection, Georgia and Maine
              Case studies   34

Table 3.1   Comparisons of 'don't know' responses to selected
              stage 1 questions, Wisconsin case study   47

Table 3.2   Comparison of 'don't know' responses for safety questions,
              Wisconsin case study   50

Table 3.3   Descriptive statistics, information effects, Wisconsin
              case study   52

Table 3.4   Logistic estimation results for stage 1 and stage 2, Wisconsin case study   54

Table 3.5   Bootstrap Estimates of Mean WTP, Wisconsin Case Study   55

Table 3.6   Description of the covariates for the econometric analysis, Wisconsin case study   57

Table 3.7   Full information subjective probability of exceeding standards and nitrate exposure models, Wisconsin case study   60

Table 3.8   WTP values for selected subjective probability and Nitrate exposure values, Wisconsin case study   62

Table 4.1   Estimates of mean willingness to pay, Pennsylvania case study   72

Table 4.2   Percentage of correct responses to information quiz, Pennsylvania case study   76

Table 4.3   Tobit regressions marginal effects, Pennsylvania Case study   78

Table 5.1   Multivariate probit analysis, Ohio case study   90

Table 5.2   Predicted vs. actual votes, Ohio case study   92

Table 5.3   Estimated median and lower bound mean (lbm) WTP ($/household, one-time payment), YNP data, Ohio case study   92

Table 5.4   Kruskal-Wallis test for multiple independent samples, Ohio case study   94

Table 5.5   Median and mean WTP ($/household), all programs Pooled, Ohio case study   96

Table 6.1   Descriptive statistics by town, MA, PA and NY benefits transfer study   108

Table 6.2   OLS regression estimates of WTP model for ground
               water protection, entire data set, MA, PA and NY
                benefits transfer study   110

Table 6.3   Measures of accuracy using policy site as base,
               various data subgroupings, MA, PA and NY benefits
               transfer study   112

Table 6.4   Accuracy improvements due to sample size for
               Direct and benefits function transfers, MA, PA and NY
               benefits transfer study   114

Table 6.5   Average percentage errors and benefit function
               equivalence, MA, PA and NY benefits transfer
               study   115

Table 6.6   Average percentage errors for individual town
               transfers for h_0^1 and h_0^2, MA, PA and NY benefits
               transfer study   116

Table 7.1   Descriptive statistics, PA, GA and ME benefits
               transfer study   128

Table 7.2   Marginal effects -probit results, PA, GA and ME
               benefits transfer study   129

Table 7.3   Marginal effects - tobit models without protests, PA,
               GA and ME benefits transfer study   132

Table 7.4   Directly estimated WTP (dollars), PG, GA and ME
               benefits transfer study   133

Table 7.5   Probit WTP estimates using functional transfers
               (dollars), PA, GA and ME benefits transfer study   133

Table 8.1   Core variable means for data used in meta-analysis
               by study, organized by study type   148

Table 8.2   Survey and elicitation effect means used in meta-
               analysis by study, organized by study type   150

Table 8.3   Estimated meta-analyses for ground water WTP
               functions   156

List of Contributors

John C. Bergstrom, Professor, Department of Agricultural and Applied Economics, The University of Georgia, Athens, Georgia, USA

Richard C. Bishop, Professor and Department Chair, Department of Agricultural and Applied Economics, University of Wisconsin, Madison, Wisconsin, USA

Kevin J. Boyle, Libra Professor of Environmental Economics, Department of Resource Economics and Policy, University of Maine, Orono, Maine, USA

Willard Delavan, Graduate Research Assistant, Department of Agricultural Economics and Rural Sociology, The Pennsylvania State University, University Park, Pennsylvania, USA

Damitha DeZoysa, Economist, Ministry of Finance, Columbo, Sri Lanka

Donald J. Epp, Professor, Department of Agricultural Economics and Rural Sociology, The Pennsylvania State University, University Park, Pennsylvania, USA

Gregory L. Poe, Associate Professor, Department of Applied Economics and Management, Cornell University, Ithaca, New York, USA, and Visiting Fellow, Jackson Environmental Institute (JEI/Centre for Social and Economics Research on the Global Environment (CSERGE), University of East Anglia, Norwich, Norfolk, UK.

John R. Powell, Senior Research Fellow, Countryside and Community Research Unit, Cheltenham and Gloucester College of Higher Education, Cheltenham, UK

Alan Randall, Professor and Department Chair, Department of Agricultural, Environmental and Development Economics, The Ohio State University, Columbus, Ohio, USA

Mitsuyasu Yabe, Director, Research Coordination Division, National Research Institute of Agricultural Economics, Ministry of Agriculture, Forestry and Fishery, Japan

Side Yu, Senior Researcher, STAPROBE, Ann Arbor, Michigan, USA

Timothy P. VandenBerg, Economist, Congressional Budget Office, Washington, DC

Preface

Many of the authors of this book including John Bergstrom, Richard Bishop, Kevin Boyle, Donald Epp, Gregory Poe and Alan Randall are members of a regional research project sponsored by the US Department of Agriculture entitled 'Benefits Transfer in Natural Resource Planning'. This project is more commonly known by its official government call number, W-133. Major objectives of the W-133 regional project include developing and applying theory and techniques for natural resource valuation and benefits transfer. In 1995, the W-133 coauthors of this book began collaborative efforts to improve and apply methodology for valuing ground water quality and testing the potential for benefits transfer as applied to ground water quality. These collaborative efforts provided the inspiration and impetus for this book. Although the applications discussed in this book focus on ground water quality, the theory and techniques discussed apply to valuation of water quality in general. Thus, the book should be of interest and relevance to people concerned with the economic valuation of water quality, whether the source of water is ground or surface water supplies.

The studies upon which this book is based were conducted with the financial support of the US Department of Agriculture and the Agricultural Experiment Stations located at Cornell University, the University of Georgia, the University of Maine, the Ohio State University, the Pennsylvania State University, and the University of Wisconsin through the W-133 regional project. **We owe a debt and give our sincere thanks to Ms. Jo Anne Norris at the University of Georgia for her dedicated and professional word processing and typesetting of the final book.**

1. Economic Value of Water Quality: Introduction and Conceptual Background

John C. Bergstrom, Kevin J. Boyle and Gregory L. Poe

INTRODUCTION

Water is one of the most ubiquitous of natural resources in terms of where it is found and the uses by living organisms. Water, of course, is an essential element of human, animal and plant life. Take away a person's food supply, and he or she may continue to live for several weeks. Take away a person's drinking water supply, and that person will be dead within a few days. Water has both quantity and quality dimensions. A person stuck on a life raft in the middle of the ocean is surrounded by an abundant quantity of water, but the salt content in sea water renders its quality unsuitable for sustaining life. The focus of this book is on valuation of water quality, rather than water quantity.

Sources of water for human use come from surface and ground water supplies. Surface water supplies include rivers, lakes, ponds and cistern catchments from rainfall. Ground water supplies include various types of aquifers located below the surface of the ground.

The quality of surface and ground water supplies in this book refers to the usefulness of the water for anthropocentric uses. This usefulness can be negatively impacted by several sources of contamination, including chemical contamination and bacterial contamination, which can directly affect human health, and attributes that affect the desirability of water as a potable source (e.g., color, taste, and smell). The highest standards for water quality are those that make it suitable for sustaining human health and life.

The valuation of 'safe' drinking water is the primary subject of this book. The valuation theory and techniques described in the book are applied to the specific case of valuing safe drinking water provided by ground water supplies. The theory and techniques, however, can be extended in a straightforward manner to valuing safe drinking water provided by surface water supplies. The theory and techniques in this book can also be applied to valuing lower levels of water quality such as 'fishable' waters, 'swimmable' waters, and 'boatable' waters and waters that sustain a healthy ecosystem (Mitchell and Carson, 1985; Carson and Mitchell, 1993).

In this book we will focus specifically on applications for valuing ground water quality. It is important to recognize, however, that the quantity and quality dimensions of ground water are interrelated. Ground water quantity and quality are in the nature of renewable stock resources (Conrad and Olson, 1992). Sustainable use of this resource requires an adequate quantity and quality of water recharge into an aquifer. If the quantity of water withdrawn from an aquifer (outflow) is greater than the quantity of water recharging into the aquifer (inflow) the stock of water in the aquifer will eventually be depleted. In addition to *quantity* depletion, the *quality* of a stock of ground water can be depleted. Ground water quality is depleted or degraded when the inflow of water recharge is contaminated from natural or anthropocentric sources. Anthropocentric sources of contamination include application of pesticides and fertilizers to agricultural fields, golf courses, and private lawns, private and municipal septic systems, underground disposal of industrial wastes, underground storage of petroleum products (for example, underground storage of gasoline at service stations), and accidental spills of chemicals and petroleum products.

Surface and ground water stocks and flows are physically interrelated. Surface water percolates through the soil to recharge underground aquifers and water from underground aquifers flows into surface water supplies through springs and wetlands. The quality of surface and ground water supplies defined over time and geographic space are intertwined. Ground water is the source of 'drinkable' water for many people throughout the world. In rural areas, private wells are the most common means for accessing ground water for drinking purposes. These wells sometimes are shallow, hand-dug wells with dirt- or rock-lined walls. Where household incomes are higher and the necessary technological services are available, private wells are more often deep, pipe-lined wells drilled mechanically by professional well-drillers. The depth of these wells varies with the characteristics of different aquifers. In many rural towns and areas, community water systems consist of a shared well operated by a private water company or a municipality. Some larger towns and cities also use ground water for municipal water systems.

Although we know people value having an uncontaminated source of drinking water, we do not generally know *how much* an uncontaminated source of water is worth to different individuals in economic value terms. Through a series of case studies, this book increases our understanding of how much people value ground water quality and why. This economic value information is important for conducting benefit-cost studies of water supply policies and programs, for informing natural resource damage assessment cases, and helping water managers to make decisions affecting their water customers. The economic value estimates reported and discussed in each of the chapters of this book have their theoretical basis in the general conceptual model of the economic value of water quality presented in the next section.

Defining the Water Quality 'Commodity' to be Valued

A basic step in the economic valuation of water quality is defining the water quality 'commodity' of interest. Water quality supports many types of economic services valued by people. In an economic valuation exercise, the water quality 'commodity' to be valued is some change in economic services brought about by a change in water quality. Bergstrom *et al.* (1996) propose a framework for identifying and valuing ground water services. This framework is adopted and revised in this section to identify a process for valuing water quality services in general.

The first step in the commodity definition process is to determine the temporal perspective of the change in economic services. If the change in economic services has already occurred, commodity definition and valuation proceeds from an *ex post* perspective. If the change in economic services is a proposed change, commodity definition and valuation proceeds from an *ex ante* perspective. Temporal considerations also include determining the time frame over which the change in quality will occur and be maintained. We also need to consider the geographical scope of water quality changes to determine the relevant regions and populations of people that will be affected by the change in quality.

The next step in the water quality definition and valuation process is to determine the baseline water quality condition and the expected water quality condition under a policy or valuation scenario. Differences between the baseline condition and expected condition define the change in water quality to be valued. In the case of proposed water quality changes, uncertainty enters the picture because human mechanisms and/or natural processes may not result in the proposed change occurring with complete certainty. In addition, it may be impossible from an *ex ante* perspective to predict baseline quality with certainty. Thus, assessment of the predicted baseline and future quality levels typically includes consideration of uncertainty and probabilities of alternative water quality changes.

Figure 1.1 summarizes the technical data required to define the water quality 'commodity' to be valued in a policy analysis. The first step is water quality monitoring (Box 1, Figure 1.1). This results in an estimate of the

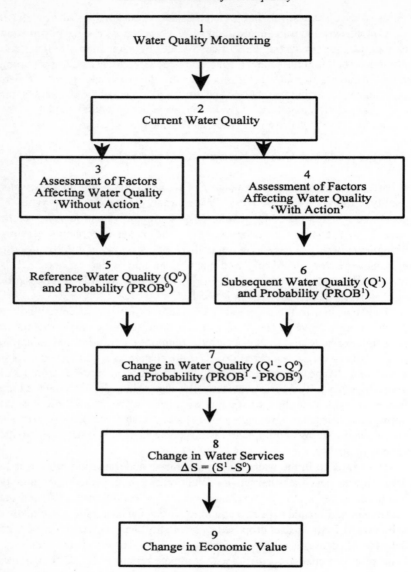

Figure 1.1. Water quality valuation process.

current or baseline level of water quality (Box 2, Figure 1.1). Changes in factors which may affect water quality in the 'without action' and 'with action' situations such as natural contamination (e.g., salt infiltration), and human-induced contamination (e.g., pesticide contamination, industrial chemical contamination) are then assessed (Boxes 3 and 4, Figure 1.1). This is the step where probabilities need to be assigned to the 'with' and 'without' action projections of water quality. The results of this assessment are estimates of the reference (e.g., 'without action') water quality level (Q^0) and the subsequent (e.g., 'with action') water quality level (Q^1), and the respective probabilities ($PROB^0$ and $PROB^1$) (Boxes 5 and 6, Figure 1.1). Given these estimates, we can define the change in water quality in the valuation scenario as ($Q^1 - Q^0$) with the appropriate adjustments for the probabilities associated with the water quality levels (Box 7, Figure 1.1). The difference ($Q^1 - Q^0$) may be greater than or less than zero depending on whether an action reduces (environmental accident) or improves (cleans up) quality.

Let S denote a vector of economic services supported by water quality where reference service levels are given by $S^0 = f(PROB^0, Q^0)$ and subsequent service levels are given by $S^1 = f(PROB^1, Q^1)$. The change in water quality services is then defined as ($S^1 - S^0$) or ΔS (Box 8, Figure 1.1). This change in water quality services will result in a change in individual utility or satisfaction and, in turn, a change in economic value (Box 9, Figure 1.1).

The steps and linkages illustrated by Boxes 1 to 7 primarily involve the work of hydrologists, geologists, engineers, soil scientists, chemists and other physical scientists and technicians. Physical scientists and other analysts, for example, must conduct careful water quality monitoring and assessments of potential contamination pathways in order to estimate current, reference and subsequent water quality levels. Examination of changes in services and human satisfaction from economic commodities takes us into the realm of human behavior. The linkage between boxes 7 and 8 involves the combined efforts of physical scientists and social scientists, including economists. Economists in particular face the challenge of measuring an appropriate money metric for individual welfare changes associated with changes in economic value in Box 9. Figure 1.1 illustrates that comprehensive valuation of water quality for policy analysis requires interaction and cooperation between physical and social scientists.

Economic Services Supported by Water Quality
High quality ground water, as well as surface water, supports many economic services. A service may have both positive and negative effects, depending upon the affected party's preferences or reference perspective. One of the major economic services supported by clean water is drinking water for human consumption. For example, contamination of ground water reduces its

usefulness as a supply of potable water and preventing ground water contamination enhances its future usefulness as a potable supply.

Relatively high water quality is also needed to support drinking water for livestock consumption and perhaps, to a lesser degree, agricultural crop irrigation. Relatively high water quality is also needed for many industrial purposes including food product processing (e.g., poultry processing). Compared to food processing, relatively lower water quality may be required to support manufactured goods production (e.g., clothing), heated water for geothermal power plants, and cooling water for other power plants. Allowing lower levels of water quality also provides opportunities for using surface and ground water resources to support waste disposal services (e.g., use of a water resource as a medium for the absorption, transport, and dilution of sewage wastes and other by-products of human economic activity).

Interrelated surface and ground water systems support the quality of surface water bodies (e.g., lakes and rivers) and wetland areas. Healthy surface water and wetland ecosystems support a variety of economic services including potable surface water, healthy aquatic ecosystems, flood control, erosion control, recreational swimming, recreational boating, recreational fishing, recreational hunting/trapping, recreational plant gathering, commercial fishing, commercial hunting/trapping, commercial plant gathering, on-site nature observation and study (e.g., bird watching), and off-site nature observation and study (e.g., viewing wildlife photos). Ground water quality may also support non-use or passive use services.

Healthy aquatic ecosystems supported by water quality may also generate broad ecosystem services and intrinsic services. Surface plants supported by high water quality (e.g., trees, grasses) in riparian and wetlands ecosystems may help to regulate local and global climate. Surface water body and wetlands ecosystems may also generate non-use or passive use services. These services, for example, would include the mental action of a person contemplating the existence of wildlife and plants in a wetlands area that the person has not visited and never plans to visit, or the services provided by high water quality for future generations.

In this book we will focus on the valuation of ground water as a quality source of potable water. The conceptual framework and valuation methods discussed can be equally used to estimate other values that individuals receive from changes in ground water quality.

ECONOMIC VALUATION APPROACHES

The challenge to economists is to translate changes in ground water quality to dollar terms. For example, consider drinking water services. Drinking water provides a flow of human health benefits. The economic value of continued health benefits is reflected by an individual's willingness to pay to consume uncontaminated water. The economic value of changes in health benefits or risks (e.g., as reflected by willingness to pay) can be measured using a valuation tool or technique such as water market demand functions (Walker and Hoehn, 1990), averting or defensive expenditures (Abdalla *et al*, 1992; Abdalla, 1994; Bartik, 1988; Harford, 1984; Vossler *et al*, 1998), damages avoided (Raucher, 1986), changes in production costs (Freeman and Harrington, 1990; Holmes, 1988; Ribaudo and Hellerstein, 1992), hedonic price method (Mendelsohn *et al.*, 1992; Polinsky and Rubinfeld, 1977; Ribaudo and Hellerstein, 1992) or stated preference methods such as the contingent valuation method or conjoint analysis (Carson and Mitchell, 1993; Caudill and Hoehn, 1992; Collins and Steinback, 1993; Edwards,1988; Jordan and Elnagheeb, 1993; Kwak *et al.* 1997; Luzar and Cosse', 1998; McClelland *et al.*, 1992; Poe, 1993; Poe, 1998; Poe and Bishop, 1999; Powell and Allee, 1991; Powell *et al.*, 1994 Shultz and Lindsay, 1990; Stevens *et al.*, 1997; Sun *et al.*, 1992).

Another service supported by water quality is the provision of drinking water for livestock and crop irrigation. A change in the quality of water used for these purposes may result in a change in the value of livestock or crops, a change in agricultural production costs, or a change in human health or health risks. The change in the value (e.g., price) of crops can be estimated using market demand functions for the crops of interest. The change in production costs can be estimated using estimated cost functions. A change in the provision of water for crop irrigation may affect human health and health risks by increasing or decreasing the amount of trace chemicals (e.g., pesticides) found on plants ingested by people. Potential techniques for measuring the economic value of this change in human health or health risks are the damages avoided approach and stated preference methods.

As indicated in the previous section, a change in surface and/or groundwater quality may result in a change in the quantity or quality of recreational fishing, hunting/trapping, or plant gathering. Potential techniques for valuing these effects include the travel cost method and stated preference methods (Bockstael *et al.*, 1987; Bockstael *et al.*, 1989; Caulkins *et al.*, 1986; Choe *et al*, 1996; Desvouges *et al.*, 1987; Freeman, 1995; Georgiou *et al.*, 1998; Greenley *et al.*, 1981; Green and Tunstall, 1991; Hayes *et al.*, 1992; Jakus *et al*, 1998; Loomis *et al.*, 1991; Magnussen, 1992; Montgomery and Needelman, 1997; Mullen and Menz, 1985; Osborn and Shulstad, 1983; Phaneuf *et al.*, 1998; Ribaudo and Epp, 1984; Russell and Vaughan, 1982; Smith and Desvouges, 1983; Sutherland, 1982; Sutherland and Walsh, 1985). The contribution of water quality to recreational and aesthetic benefits of water may also be reflected in property values and measured by the hedonic price method (Epp and Al-Ani, 1979; Malone and Barrows, 1990; Steinnes, 1992; Boyle *et al.*, 1999). Other potential effects of a change in the quality of surface and/or ground water quality is a change in the value or costs of commercial fish harvest, commercial hunting/trapping harvest, or commercial plant harvest. The economic value of these effects can be estimated using cost functions or market demand functions.

The effects of changes in non-use or passive use services are some of the most difficult effects to value monetarily. A change in non-use or passive use services results in a direct change in personal utility or satisfaction, that is not unlikely to be reveled by personal consumption of water. The most viable techniques for measuring these effects are stated preference methods (Greenley *et al.*, 1981; Mitchell and Carson, 1985; Greenley *et al.*, 1985).

A complete valuation of water-quality services will involve measuring the economic value of the effects of all relevant changes in ground water services discussed in the previous section. In practice, many different valuation tools and techniques will be used to accomplish this complete valuation. The choice of a valuation tool or technique depends on many factors including theoretical appropriateness, estimation robustness, ease of data collection, time and budget constraints, and professional judgement and preference.

GENERAL MODEL OF THE ECONOMIC VALUE OF WATER QUALITY

As noted above, many changes affect the probability that ground water is contaminated and, hence, its suitability as a potable water supply. Under conditions of uncertainty, option price is the appropriate welfare measure (Freeman, 1995). Certainty is just a special case of this conceptualization where the known conditions occur with certainty. The option price definition used here includes both use and non-use values for changes in water quality.

Following Boyle *et al.* (1994), option price for water quality is defined generally in a utility difference framework as:

$$\sum_{h=1}^{N} PROB_{w,j}^{h} V_{j}(Q_{w,j}^{h}, P_{j}, SP_{j}, I_{j} - OP_{j}; H_{j}) =$$

$$\sum_{h=1}^{N} PROB_{wo,j}^{h} V_{j}(Q_{wo,j}^{h}, P_{j}, SP_{j}, I_{j}; H_{j})$$

(1.1)

where OP_{j} is individual j's option price or willingness to pay for an action that changes the probability that water is contaminated; $V_{j}(.)$ represents individual j's indirect utility function; $Q_{w,j}^{h}$ represents a general or specific water quality level in the 'with action' scenario;, $PROB_{w,j}^{h}$ is the probability of the 'with action' scenario conditions occurring; $Q_{wo,j}^{h}$ represents a general or specific water quality level in the 'without action' scenario; $PROB_{wo,j}^{h}$ is the probability of the 'without action' scenario conditions occurring; I_{j} represents household income for individual j net of taxes and any averting expenditures to avoid unsafe water; P_{j} is the price of water faced by individual j; SP_{j} represents substitute prices of water faced by individual j; and H_j represents various non-income characteristics of individual j's household.

Solving 1.1 for OP implies the following general bid function:

$$OP_j = f\,(\Delta Q^h_j,\ \Delta PROB^h_j,\ \Delta P_j,\ \Delta SP_j\,|\,I_j,\ H_j\,), \tag{1.2}$$

where, ΔQ^h_j represents the change in specific or general level of water quality; $\Delta PROB^h_j$ represents the change in probability of subsequent or target conditions occurring with and without action; ΔP_j represents the change in price of water from primary supplies; ΔSP_j represents the change in price of substitute sources of water, I_j and H_j are as defined previously.

In (1.1), the terms $Q^h_{w,j}$ and $Q^h_{wo,j}$ refer to the with action and without action water quality levels. In (1.1) and (1.2), water quality levels are indexed on individual j to reflect the fact that with and without action water quality levels may differ across individuals and households. Differences in water quality levels across individuals and households may be especially prevalent in regions where most individuals and households obtain drinking water from private wells where differing levels of averting mechanisms are utilized.

In (1.1), $PROB^h_{w,j}$ represents the probability of the 'with action' conditions occurring. Suppose that the action being considered is a water quality protection program, policy or averting practices such as installing a home water filter. Desired outcomes of these actions may include protection of 'safe' drinking water quality levels or remediation of 'unsafe' drinking water levels. Because public or private water quality protection or remediation actions may not be 100% effective, potential values of $PROB^h_{w,j}$ in (1.1) range from 1 to 0.

As mentioned in the previous paragraph, the desired outcome of public or private actions may be to protect or remediate certain water quality levels. In the case of water quality protection, it is not 100% certain that water will become contaminated without water quality protection action. In the case of water quality remediation, there is likely to be a positive probability of water quality improving without water quality remediation action. For example, natural processes over time may cleanse contaminates from a water source. Thus, $PROB^h_{wo,j}$ in (1.1) can also range from 1 to 0.

In (1.1) and (1.2), probabilities in the with and without action scenarios are indexed on individual j to indicate, for example, that the probabilities of certain 'safe' and 'unsafe' water quality levels occurring with and without public or private protection or remediation action may differ across individuals and households. As discussed in more detail in several chapters of this book, *subjective* with and without action water quality probabilities can be held by individuals. We would expect subjective probabilities to differ across individuals because of differences in information about contamination. Objective with and without action water quality probabilities may also differ across individuals and households because of different personal averting practices or non-uniform spatial and/or temporal effectiveness of public water quality protection or remediation policies and programs.

The general conceptual model summarized by (1.1) and (1.2) indicates that the economic value of water quality to individual j is influenced by the socioeconomic characteristics of individual j. These socioeconomic characteristics include indicators of tastes and preferences such as age and education, and indicators of environmental and public good attitudes such as the priorities an individual places on public provision of various goods and services. The model suggests that option price may also be influenced by differences in the prices of water from primary and substitute sources in the with and without action scenarios.

Application of the general conceptual model described above is illustrated next in this chapter through several stylistic examples. Several of these applications are illustrated empirically by the case studies discussed in this book. The first set of examples considers cases where specific levels of water quality are defined.

Water Quality Changes

Q^h in (1.1) and (1.2) may represent *specific* levels of contaminants in water. For simplicity, assume two specific levels $Q^1_j = X_j$ and $Q^2_j = Y_j$ with $X_j > Y_j$ and option price represents willingness to pay to improve water quality from Y_j to X_j. Assume also that $PROB^1_{w,j}$ and $PROB^2_{w,j}$ represent the probability of water quality levels X_j and Y_j occurring in the 'with action' scenario respectively, and $PROB^1_{wo,j}$ and $PROB^2_{wo,j}$ represent the probability of water quality levels X_j and Y_j occurring in the 'without action' scenario, respectively. In this example, the general model becomes:

$$PROB^1_{w,j} \ V_j(X_j, P_j, SP_j, I_j\text{-}OP_j; H_j) + PROB^2_{w,j} \ V_j(Y_j, P_j, SP_j, I_j\text{-}OP_j; H_j) =$$
$$PROB^1_{wo,j} \ V_j(X_j, P_j, SP_j, I_j; H_j) + PROB^2_{wo,j} \ V_j(Y_j, P_j, SP_j, I_j; H_j) \qquad (1.3)$$

or in terms of the bid function,

$$OP = f(\Delta Q_j, \Delta PROB^1_j, \Delta PROB^2_j, \Delta P_j, \Delta SP_j | I_j, H_j), \qquad (1.4)$$

where ΔQ_j represents $X_j - Y_j$; $\Delta PROB^1_j$ represents the change in the probability of X_j water quality level occurring with and without the protection or remediation action; and $\Delta PROB^2_j$ is the change in the probability of Y_j water quality level occurring with and without protection or remediation action.

The economic value of water quality in (1.3) and (1.4) is defined assuming two possible levels of water quality in the 'with' and 'without' action scenarios. In reality, there may be more than two possible water quality levels that could occur with and without public or private protection or remediation action. Equations (1.3) and (1.4) can be generalized to include whatever distribution of water quality levels and associated probabilities may occur in the 'with' and 'without' action scenarios.

Consider next the special case where the higher level of water quality, X_j, will occur with certainty in the 'with action' scenario and the lower level of water quality, Y_j, will occur with certainty in the 'without action' scenario implying that: $PROB^1_{w,j} = 1$; $PROB^1_{wo,j} = 0$; $PROB^2_{w,j} = 0$; and $PROB^2_{wo,j} = 1$. In this special case, (1.3) becomes:

$$V_j(X_j, P_j, SP_j, I_j - WTP_j; H_j) = V_j(Y_j, P_j, SP_j, I_j; H_j) \qquad (1.5)$$

and (1.4) becomes:

$$WTP_j = f(\Delta Q_j, \Delta P_j, \Delta SP_j | I_j, H_j), \qquad (1.6)$$

where, ΔQ_j defines a specific change in water quality, and WTP_j representing willingness to pay under certainty replaces OP_j (which represents willingness to pay under uncertainty). For example, if $X_j = 5$ milligrams per liter content of nitrates in drinking water for individual j, and $Y_j = 15$ milligrams per liter content of nitrates in drinking water for individual j, WTP_j in (1.6) would represent individual j's willingness to pay under certainty to reduce the content of nitrates in drinking water by 10 milligrams per liter.

General Water Quality Changes
In (1.1), Q^h_j may be in the nature of a general indicator variable for 'safe' vs. 'unsafe' levels of water quality. For example, assume 'safe' drinking water is indicated by $Q^1_j = 1$ and 'unsafe' drinking water is indicated by $Q^2_j = 0$, and OP represents willingness-to-pay for general water safety. The general water quality valuation model then becomes:

$$PROB^1_{w,j} V_j(Q^1_j; P_j, SP_j, I_j - OP_j; H_j) + PROB^2_{w,j} V_j(Q^2_j, P_j, SP_j, I_j - OPj; H_j) =$$
$$PROB^1_{wo,j} V_j(Q^1_j, P_j, SP_j, I_j; H_j) + PROB^2_{wo,j} V_j(Q^2_j, P_j, SP_j, I_j; H_j) \qquad (1.7a)$$

or,

$$PROB^1_{w,j} V_j(1, P_j, SP_j, I_j - OP_j; H_j) + PROB^2_{w,j} V_j(0, P_j, SP_j, I_j - OP_j; H_j) =$$
$$PROB^1_{wo,j} V_j(1, P_j, SP_j, I_j; H_j) + PROB^2_{wo,j} V_j(0, P_j, SP_j, I_j; H_j \qquad (1.7b)$$

which further reduces to,

$$PROB^1_{w,j} V_j(1, P_j, SP_j, I_j - OP_j; H_j) = PROB^1_{wo,j} V_j(1, P_j, SP_j, I_j; H_j) \qquad (1.7c)$$

The bid function implied by (1.7) is specified generally as:

$$OP_j = f(\Delta PROB^1_j, \Delta P_j, \Delta SP_j | I_j, H_j) \qquad (1.8)$$

where, $\Delta PROB^1_j$ is the change in probability that water will be 'safe' to drink with and without public or private protection or remediation action.

As an example of valuing general water quality changes, suppose the valuation problem is concerned with measuring OP for a ground water protection program that will provide 'safe' drinking water with a 90% probability. Suppose that without the program, the probability of drinking water remaining 'safe' is 25%. Q^h has two levels: let $Q^1 = 1$ represent 'safe' drinking water, and $Q^2 = 0$ represent 'unsafe' drinking water. The general conceptual model becomes:

$$PROB^1_{w,j} V_j(Q^1, P_j, SP_j, I_j - OP_j; H_j) + PROB^2_{w,j} V_j(Q^2, P_j, SP_j, I_j - OP_j; H_j) =$$
$$PROB^1_{wo,j} V_j(Q^1, P_j, SP_j, I_j; H_j) + PROB^2_{wo,j} V_j(Q^2, P_j, SP_j, I_j; H_j) \qquad (1.9a)$$

or,

$$(.90) V_j(1, P_j, SP_j, I_j - OP_j; H_j) + (.10) V_j(0, P_j, SP_j, I_j - OP_j; H_j) =$$
$$(.25) V_j(1, P_j, SP_j, I_j; H_j) + (.75) V_j(0, P_j, SP_j, I_j; H_j) \qquad (1.9b)$$

which reduces to,

$$(.90) V_j(1, P_j, SP_j, I_j - OP_j; H_j) = (.25) V_j(1, P_j, SP_j, I_j; H_j) \qquad (1.9c)$$

In this special case, OP_j would represent an individual j's willingness-to-pay for a program improves the probability of drinking water remaining 'safe' by $.65 = .90 - .25$.

ORGANIZATION OF THE BOOK

The general conceptual model discussed in this chapter suggests the underlying determinants of the economic value of water quality to different individuals. The economic value of water quality can be estimated using economic valuation techniques including the contingent valuation method as shown in the USA case studies discussed in this book. In Chapter 2, Bergstrom *et al.* discuss a case study of ground water valuation in the states of Georgia and Maine focusing on determinants of ground water quality values including subjective supply probabilities. In Chapter 3, Poe and Bishop discuss the importance of information in the ground water valuation process in the context of a state of Wisconsin case study. Epp and Delavan discuss a Pennsylvania ground water valuation case study in Chapter 4 that parallels the Georgia and Maine study from Chapter 2, providing corroborating results and additional insights into the determinants of ground water values. Using an Ohio case study, valuation of enhancements of ground water, surface water, and wetlands provided by the same policy are discussed by Randall *et al.* in Chapter 5. The possibilities and problems associated with benefits transfer of ground water quality value estimates are discussed by VandenBerg *et al.* in Chapter 6 and Delavan and Epp in Chapter 7. Meta analysis results that provide further insights on the determinants of ground water quality values are discussed by Poe *et al.* in Chapter 8. In Chapter 9, Boyle *et al.* summarize the major implications of the topics and studies discussed in this book.

REFERENCES

Abdalla, C.W., B.A. Roach, and D.J. Epp (1992), 'Valuing environmental quality changes using averting expenditures: an application to groundwater contamination,' *Land Economics,* **68**: 163-9.

Abdalla, C.W. (1994), 'Groundwater values from avoidance cost studies: implications for policy and future research,' *American Journal of Agricultural Economics*, **76**(5):1062-7.

Bartik, T.J. (1988), 'Evaluating the benefits of non-marginal reductions in pollution using information on defensive expenditures,' *Journal of Environmental Economics and Management,* **15**:111-27.

Bergstrom, John C., Kevin J. Boyle, Charles A. Job, and Mary Jo Kealy (1996), 'Assessing the economic benefits of ground water for environmental policy decisions,' *Journal of the American Water Resources Association,* **32**(2):279-91.

Bockstael, N.E., W.M. Hanemann, and C.L. Kling (1987), 'Estimating the value of water quality improvements in a recreational demand framework.' *Water Resources Research,* **23**(5): 951-60.

Bockstael, N. E., K.E. McConnell, and I.E. Strand (1989), 'Measuring the benefits of improvements in water quality: the Chesapeake Bay,' *Marine Resource Economics*, **6**(1): 1-18.

Boyle, K.J., P. Joan Poor, and Laura O. Taylor (1999), 'Estimating the demand for protecting freshwater lakes from eutrophication,' *American Journal of Agricultural Economics,* **81**(5):1118-22.

Carson, R.T. and R.C. Mitchell (1993), 'The value of clean water: the public's willingness to pay for boatable, fishable, and swimmable quality water,' *Water Resources Research,* **29**(7): 2445-54.

Caudill, J.D. and J.P. Hoehn (1992), 'The economic valuation of groundwater pollution policies: the role of subjective risk perception,' Staff Paper No. 91-11, Department of Agricultural Economics, Michigan State University.

Caulkins, P.P., R.C. Bishop, and N.W. Bouwes, Sr. (1986), 'The travel cost model for lake recreation: a comparison of two methods for incorporating site quality and substitution effects,' *American Journal of Agricultural Economics,* **68**(2): 291-7.

Choe, K.A., D. Whittington, and D.T. Lauria (1996), 'The economic benefits of surface water quality improvements in developing countries: a case study of Davao, Philippines,' *Land Economics,* **72**(4): 519-37.

Collins, A.R. and S. Steinback (1993), 'Rural household response to water contamination in West Virginia,' *Water Resources Bulletin,* **29**(2):199-209.

Conrad, J. M. and L. J. Olson (1992), 'The economics of a stock pollutant,' *Environmental and Resource Economics,* **2**: 245-58.

Desvouges, W.H., V.K. Smith, and A. Fisher (1987), 'Option price estimates for water quality improvements: a contingent valuation study for the Monongahela River,' *Journal of Environmental Economics and Management,* **14**:248-67.

Edwards, S.F. (1988), 'Option prices for groundwater protection,' *Journal of Environmental Economics and Management,* **15**: 475-87.

Epp, D.J. and K.S. Al-Ani (1979), 'The effect of water quality on rural nonfarm residential property values,' *American Journal of Agricultural Economics,* **61**(3): 529-34.

Freeman, A.M. III (1995), 'The benefits of water quality improvements for marine recreation: a review of the empirical evidence,' *Marine Resource Economics,* **10**(4): 385-406.

Freeman, A.M., III and W. Harrington (1990), 'Measuring welfare values of productivity changes,' *Southern Economic Journal,* **56**:892-904.

Georgiou, S., I.H. Langford, I.J. Bateman, and R.K. Turner (1998), 'Determinants of individuals' willingness to pay for perceived reductions in environmental health risks: a case study of bathing water quality,' *Environment and Planning A,* **30**(4): 577-94.

Green, C. H. and S.M. Tunstall (1991), 'The evaluation of river water quality improvements by the contingent valuation method,' *Applied Economics,* **23**(7): 1135-46.

Greenley, D.A., R.G. Walsh, and R.A.Young (1981), 'Option value: empirical evidence from a case study of recreation and water quality,' *Quarterly Journal of Economics,* **96**(4): 657-73.

Greenley, D.A., R.G.Walsh, and R.A. Young (1985), 'Option value: empirical evidence from a case study of recreation and water quality: reply,' *Quarterly Journal of Economics,* **10**(1): 295-9.

Harford, J.D. (1984), 'Averting behavior and the benefits of reduced soiling,' *Journal of Environmental Economics and Management,* **11**:296-302.

Hayes, K.M., T.J. Tyrrell, and G. Anderson (1992), 'Estimating the benefits of water quality improvements in the Upper Narragansett Bay,' *Marine Resource Economics,* **7**(1): 75-85.

Holmes, T.P. (1988), 'Soil erosion and water treatment, *Land Economics* **64**:356-66.

Jakus, P.M., D. Dadakas, and J.M. Fly (1998), 'Fish consumption advisories: incorporating angler-specific knowledge, habits, and catch rates in a site choice model,' *American Journal of Agricultural Economics*, **80**(5): 1019-24.

Jordan, J.L. and A.H. Elnagheeb (1993), 'Willingness to pay for improvements in drinking water quality,' *Water Resources Research*, **29**: 237-45.

Kwak, S., J. Lee, and C.S. Russell (1997), 'Dealing with censored data from contingent valuation surveys: symmetrically-trimmed least squares estimation,' *Southern Economic Journal*, **63**(3): 743-50.

Loomis, J.B., W.M. Hanemann, B.J. Kanninen, and T. Wegge (1991), 'Willingness to pay to protect wetlands and reduce wildlife contamination from agricultural drainage,' in Dinar, A. and D. Zilberman (ed.) *The Economics and Management of Water and Drainage in Agriculture*, Boston: Kluwer Academic.

Luzar, E. J., and K.J. Cossé (1998), 'Willingness to pay or intention to pay: the attitude-behavior relationship in contingent valuation,' *Journal of Socio-Economics*, **27**(3): 427-44.

Magnussen, K. (1992), 'Valuation of reduced water pollution using the contingent valuation method–testing for mental accounts and amenity misspecification,' in Navrud, Stale (ed.) *Pricing the European Environment*, Oslo: Scandinavian University Press; distributed by Oxford University Press, New York, pp. 195-230.

Malone, P. and R. Barrows (1990), 'Groundwater pollution effect on residential property values, Portage County, Wisconsin,' *Journal of Soil and Water Conservation*, **45**:346-8.

McClelland, G.H., W.D.Schulze, J.K.Lazo, D.M. Waldman, J.K.Doyle, S.R.Elliott, and J.R.Irwin (1992), 'Methods for measuring non-use values: a contingent valuation study of groundwater cleanup,' Final Report, Office of Policy, Planning, and Evaluation, US Environmental Protection Agency, Cooperative Agreement #CR-815183.

Mendelsohn, Robert, Daniel Hellerstein, Michael Hugenin, Robert Unsworth, and Richard Brazee (1992), 'Measuring hazardous waste damages with panel models,' *Journal of Environmental Economics and Management*, **22**:259-71.

Mitchell, R.C. and R.T. Carson (1985), 'Option value: empirical evidence from a case study of recreation and water quality: comment,' *Quarterly Journal of Economics*, **10**(1): 291-4.

Montgomery, M. and M. Needelman (1997), 'The welfare effects of toxic contamination in freshwater fish,' *Land Economics*, **77**(Aug): 211-23.

Mullen, J.K. and F.C. Menz (1985), 'The effect of acidification damages on the economic value of the Adirondack fishing to New York anglers,' *American Journal of Agricultural Economics*, **67**(1):112-9.

Osborn, C.T. and R.N. Shulstad (1983), 'Controlling agricultural soil loss in Arkansas' North Lake Chicot watershed: an analysis of benefits,' *Journal of Soil & Water Conservation*, Nov.-Dec.:509-12.

Phaneuf, D.J., C.L. Kling and J.A. Herriges (1998), 'Valuing water quality improvements using revealed preference methods when corner solutions are present,' *American Journal of Agricultural Economics*, **80**(5):1025-31.

Poe, G.L. and R.C. Bishop (1999), 'Valuing the incremental benefits of groundwater protection when exposure levels are known,' *Environmental and Resource Economics*, **13**(3): 341-67.

Poe, G.L. (1993), 'Information, risk perceptions and contingent values: the case of nitrates in groundwater,' Unpublished Dissertation, Department of Agricultural Economics, University of Wisconsin-Madison.

Poe, G.L. (1998), 'Valuation of groundwater quality using a contingent valuation-damage function approach,' *Water Resources Research*, **34**(12): 3627-33.

Polinsky, M. and D. Rubinfeld (1977), 'Property values and the benefits of environmental improvement: theory and measurement, *Public Economics and the Quality of Life*, Baltimore: Johns Hopkins Univ. Press.

Powell, J. R. and D. J. Allee (1991), 'The estimation of groundwater protection benefits and their utilization by local government decision-makers' , US Geological Survey, award number 14-08-0001.

Powell, J.R., D.J. Allee, and C. McClintock (1994), 'Groundwater protection benefits and local community planning: impact of contingent valuation information,' *American Journal of Agricultural Economics*, **76**(5):1068-75.

Raucher, Robert L. (1986), 'The benefits and costs of policies related to groundwater contamination,' *Land Economics*, **62**(1):33-45.

Ribaudo, M.O. and D.J. Epp (1984), 'The importance of sample discrimination in using the travel cost method to estimate the benefits of improved water quality,' *Land Economics*, **60**(4): 397-403.

Ribaudo, Marc O. and Daniel Hellerstein (1992), 'Estimating water quality benefits: theoretical and methodological issues,' USDA ERS Technical Bulletin Number 1808.

Russell, C.S. and W.J. Vaughan (1982), 'The national recreational fishing benefits of water pollution control,' *Journal of Environmental Economics and Management*, **9**:328-54.

Shultz, S.D. and B.E. Lindsay (1990), 'The willingness to pay for groundwater protection,' *Water Resources Research*, **26**:1869-75.

Smith, V.K. and W.H. Desvouges (1983), 'The generalized travel-cost model and water quality benefits: a reconsideration,' *Southern Economic Journal*, **59**(3):259-78.

Steinnes, D.N. (1992), 'Measuring the economic value of water quality: the case of lakeshore land,' *Annals of Regional Science*, **26**(2): 171-6.

Stevens, T.H., C. Barrett, and C.E. Willis (1997), 'Conjoint analysis of groundwater protection programs,' *Agricultural and Resource Economics Review*, **26**(2): 229-36.

Sun, H., J.C. Bergstrom, and J.H. Dorfman (1992), 'Estimating the benefits of groundwater contamination control,' *Southern Journal of Agricultural Economics*, **24**(2):63-70.

Sutherland, R.J. (1982). 'A regional approach to estimating recreation benefits of improved water quality,' *Journal of Environmental Economics and Management*, **9**(3): 229-47.

Sutherland, R.J., and R.G. Walsh (1985), 'Effect of distance on the preservation value of water quality,' *Land Economics*, **61**(3): 281-91.

Vossler, C.A., J. Espey, and W.D. Shaw (1998), 'Trick or treat: an offer to obtain metered water,' *Journal of the American Water Resources Association*, **34**(5):1213-20.

Walker, David R. and John P. Hoehn (1990), 'The economic damages of groundwater contamination in small rural communities: an application to nitrates,' *North Central Journal of Agricultural Economics*, **12**(1):47-56.

2. Determinants of Ground Water Quality Values: Georgia and Maine Case Studies

John C. Bergstrom, Kevin J. Boyle, and Mitsuyasu Yabe

INTRODUCTION

A number of previous studies have estimated the economic value of ground water quality using nonmarket valuation techniques (Bergstrom and Dorfman, 1994; Edwards, 1988; Hanley, 1989; Jordan and Elnagheeb ,1993; McClelland *et al.*, 1992; Poe and Bishop, 1993; Powell, 1991; Shultz and Lindsay, 1990). These studies have increased our understanding of water quality values, but there is still much to be learned about how various factors influence such values. For example, the effects of risk on water quality values are still not well understood, especially with respect to subjective risk perceptions. The purpose of this chapter is to build upon the general water quality valuation model presented in Chapter 1 of this book and previous ground water quality valuation studies by assessing the determinants of ground water quality values focusing on subjective risk assessment. Empirical valuation equations and water quality estimates are reported and compared across the states of Georgia and Maine, USA.

CONCEPTUAL CONSIDERATIONS

The general theory of water quality values presented in Chapter 1 (this book) suggests that the economic value of a change in water quality can be measured by option price defined generally as:

$$OP = f(\Delta Q, \Delta PROB \mid I, H, Z) \tag{2.1}$$

where OP represents option price for a change in water quality; ΔQ represents the change in water quality; $\Delta PROB$ represents the change in risk of suffering adverse effects of poor water quality; I represents household income; H represents a variety of non-income household characteristics (e.g., family structure, sources of water, general behavior and preferences); and Z represents research method effects. Research method effects include data collection and analysis methods selected by researchers such as the value elicitation procedure (e.g., open-ended questions), culling of observations (e.g., elimination of outliers and 'protest bidders') and mean value estimation procedure. The risk referred to in Equation 2.1 is people's perceived subjective expectations of an adverse health effect from ground water contamination. While it is possible to monitor wells for contaminated ground water, it is difficult to obtain objective calculations of the resultant health risks. The household risks vary from household to household based on averting behavior and the demographic composition of each household. Moreover, when respondents answer averting behavior and contingent-valuation questions, as used in the current study, we believe their responses to the valuation question are based on their perceptions of the change in risk (changes in subjective risk).

Previous to the studies reported in this book, relatively few studies of ground water quality values have included a risk term in the valuation equation (Edwards, 1988; Sun *et al.* 1992). What are the implications of omitting a risk assessment variable from Equation 2.1? From a theoretical perspective, Equation 2.1 would be misspecified which could lead to several empirical estimation problems and policy application errors.

If the omitted relevant variable is correlated with the remaining variables, then estimates of the coefficients on the remaining variables are generally biased and inconsistent. Biased coefficient estimates can, in turn, lead to biased estimates of option price and potentially flawed policy decisions. For example, public and private decisions to invest in water quality protection or remediation programs may be based, at least in part, on the outcome of benefit-cost analysis. Option price estimates with a downward bias may lead to under investment in protection or remediation programs. Conversely, option price estimates with an upward bias may lead to overinvestment in protection or remediation programs. Omitting $\Delta PROB$ from the estimation can also prevent the derivation of marginal welfare changes for alternative reductions in risk. Excluding $\Delta PROB$ simply provides one welfare estimate for the average reduction in risk.

Valuation Model

Suppose a program is proposed in a region for protecting ground water from potential contamination from agricultural fertilizers, industrial wastes, residential septic tanks, or some other human source. The indirect utility function of individuals in the region before the protection program has been implemented is specified as:

$$V^0 = V (Q^0, I|H), \tag{2.2}$$

where Q^0 is the 'without policy' level of water quality; I is an individual's current household income; and H represents other household characteristics. The utility function of individuals in the region after the protection program has been implemented is specified as:

$$V^1 = V (Q^1, I-C|H), \tag{2.3}$$

where Q^1 represents the 'with policy' level of water quality; C is the per household cost of the protection program; and all other variables are as defined for Equation 2.2.

We model Q here as a binary variable. Suppose that the ground water protection program is designed to maintain the level of potential contaminants at or below government health standards. If the program is implemented and successfully protects ground water quality, then $Q^1 = 1$. If the program is implemented but does not successfully protect ground water, then $Q^1 = 0$. This threshold approach presumes people are only concerned with whether their water is above or below the government standard for contamination. Any water source that does not meet the government standard is contaminated and $Q^1 = 0$. Under these conditions, with uncertain ground water quality, we can define the expected change in indirect utility with and without a protection program as:

$$\Delta V = [PROB^1 V(1, I-OP|H) + (1-PROB^1) V(0, I-OP|H)] - [PROB^0 V(1, I|H) + (1-PROB^0) V(0, I|H)], \tag{2.4}$$

where $PROB^1$ is an individual's subjective probability that ground water quality will meet government standards after the protection program is implemented; and $PROB^0$ is an individual's subjective probability that ground water will meet government standards if the protection program is not implemented. Maximum option price (OP) is the reduction in income that will equate Equation 2.4 to zero. If we set Equation 2.4 equal to zero and solve for OP, the result is the general option price equation:

$$OP = f (\Delta H_2OSAFETY| I, H,Z). \tag{2.5}$$

where $\Delta H_2 OSAFETY$ is a variable that combines ΔQ and $\Delta PROB$ in Equation 2.1 to define a respondent's subjective perception of the likelihood of receiving 'safe' drinking water with and without the protection program[1]; Z refers to elements of the research methodology used to estimate OP; and I and H are as defined previously.

EMPIRICAL STUDY

The study areas considered for the empirical estimation and comparison of option price equations and mean values were Dougherty County, Georgia and Aroostook County, Maine. The particular source of potential ground water contamination considered was nitrates from agricultural practices. In Dougherty County, regardless of private well or public water system resources, close to 100% of people get their drinking water from underground water supplies. At the time of this study, ground water quality monitoring data from the Georgia Department of Natural Resources, Environmental Protection Division indicates that currently about 98% of public and private ground water supplies in Dougherty County had nitrate levels below the US federal government safety standard of 10 milligrams NO_3-N per liter. In Aroostook County, 83% of people get their drinking water from underground water supplies. Also at the time of this study, ground water quality monitoring data from the Maine Department of Environmental Protection indicated that about 87% of public and private ground water supplies in Aroostook County have nitrate levels which are below the federal safety standard of 10 milligrams NO_3 - N per liter.

A contingent valuation (CV) field survey was conducted to measure option price for a ground water protection program in the study counties. A standardized questionnaire was used in each state. The questionnaire was divided into four sections. The first section asked questions about a respondent's residence, experiences and concerns with ground water quality and other public issues. The second section began by presenting information on ground water supplies, potential contamination sources, potential health effects of nitrate contamination, and questions to assess background knowledge of these issues.

The third section presented the valuation scenario and question. The valuation scenario described a proposed ground water protection program designed to keep the level of nitrates in ground water supplies in the future at or below the US federal health standard. A dichotomous-choice (DC) valuation question asked if a respondent would vote to support the proposed program given a specified cost to their household in the form of a one-time special tax payment. The valuation question was stated in the questionnaire as follows:

*The costs of the program would have to be paid by you and other citizens. The program will be funded by a **special tax**. Thus, paying for the program would reduce the amount of money you have to spend on the other goods and services. If it is approved by voters, the program, including the special tax, will be in effect for 10 years only.*

*If the program of providing technical and financial assistance to individuals and groups interested in protecting ground water from potential nitrate contamination were placed on the next ballot, would you vote for the program if the **special tax needed to fund the program cost your household** ____ **per year for 10 years** ? (Circle one number)*

1. *Yes - I would vote in favor of the program.*
2. *No - I would vote against the program.*

Survey Procedures

The survey was conducted from September, 1996 to March, 1997; 1050 households in Maine and 1049 households in Georgia were randomly selected from county registered voter list and telephone directories. Both samples were purchased from Survey Sampling, Inc.

The samples in each state were further divided into eight subgroups, which were assigned to receive one of eight offer amounts for the dichotomous choice (DC) valuation question. The offer amounts were $25, $50, $75, $100, $150, $200, $350 and $500, respectively. These offer prices were based on meta-analysis of ground water values from previous studies (Boyle *et al.*, 1994). The alternative offer prices were written into the valuation question shown above.

An initial questionnaire in Georgia was sent to all households in the sample. One week later a reminder postcard was sent to all households again. Three weeks later the first follow-up cover letter and replacement questionnaire were sent to all non-respondents. One month later a second follow-up cover letter and replacement questionnaire were sent to all non-respondents. Parallel procedures were followed in Maine. A third cover letter and replacement questionnaire were sent to the Georgia sample to help boost the response rate. Of 1,049 questionnaires sent out in Georgia, 262 (25%) were undeliverable because of wrong address, leaving an adjusted sample frame size of 787. Four hundred and seventeen questionnaires were returned for an response rate of 53%. Also of 1,050 surveys sent out in Maine, 130 (12%) were undeliverable because of wrong addresses, leaving an adjusted sample size of 920. Four hundred and eighty-six questionnaires were returned for a response rate of 53%.

Ad hoc Option Price Equations

One set of option-price equations estimated for the Georgia and Maine data sets were based on *ad hoc* specifications of Equation 2.4 and 2.5. In order to model the 'yes' or 'no' responses to the DC valuation question presented in the CV questionnaire, the probability of a 'yes' response was modeled as:

$$Pr(Yes) = \Phi (\Delta V) \tag{2.6}$$

where $\Phi(.)$ is the standard probit function. Based on Equation 2.4, ΔV in Equation 2.6 was defined as:

$$\Delta V = B_0 + B_1 BID + B_2 \, \Delta H_2 OSAFETY + B_3 I + B_4 PROACTIVE + B_5 CHILDREN \, PRESENT + B_6 CONCERN + B_7 PRIVATE \, WATER, \tag{2.7a}$$

and,

$$\Delta V = B_0 + B_1 BID + B_2 \, \Delta H_2 OSAFETY \tag{2.7b}$$

where BID represents the offer amount or cost of protection program; $\Delta H_2 OSAFETY$ represents a respondent's subjective estimate of the change in probability of water remaining 'safe' to drink with a protection program; I represents household income; PROACTIVE represents current practices in a household conducted to reduce exposure to contaminated water (1 if actions taken to reduce exposure; 0 otherwise); CHILDREN PRESENT represents the number of children 13 years or younger in a household, CONCERN measures an individual's level of concern over ground water contamination problems; and PRIVATE WATER indicates whether household drinking water is from a public or private source (1 if private source; 0 otherwise). Equation 2.6b omits the household income and characteristic variables included in 2.6a.

Equations 2.4 and 2.5 indicate that a risk assessment variable should be included in empirical option price equations. Water quality studies, however, do not always include consideration of objective or subjective probabilities of water contamination with and without water quality protection programs. To examine the effects of omitting a risk assessment variable, Equation 2.6 was also estimated defining ΔV as:

$$\Delta V = B_0 + B_1 \, BID + B_3 I + B_4 \, PROACTIVE + B_5 \, CHILDREN \, PRESENT + B_6 \, CONCERN + B_7 \, PRIVATE \, WATER, \tag{2.7c}$$

where $\Delta H_2 OSAFETY$ is omitted.

All models were also estimated with and without 'protest bidders.' In the questionnaire, the DC valuation question was followed up by an open-ended valuation question. A respondent who indicated a zero willingness to pay in the open-ended question was asked to provide a reason. A zero-bidder who indicated that his or her zero bid was in the nature of a 'protest' to the valuation question or scenario were considered protest bidders. More detailed discussions of protest bidders and reasons for excluding these bidders from welfare estimates can be found in Mitchell and Carson (1989).

Mean values for the independent variables in Equation 2.6 are shown in Table 2.1. Mean option price was estimated from each equation using the Hanemann (1984) integration approach allowing only for non-negative bids, and the Cameron (1988) direct equation approach that allows for negative bids.

Utility Theoretic Approach
Option price equations and mean option price were also estimated using a utility theoretic approach. To implement this approach, an indirect utility function was specified with the following linear functional form:

$$V = b_0 + b_1 I + b_2 Q. \tag{2.8}$$

This linear specification assumes people are risk neutral. Given Equation 2.7, the utility difference with and without the ground water protection program is defined as:

$$\Delta V = [PROB^1 (b_0 + b_2 + b_1 (I\text{-}OP)) + (1\text{-}PROB^1) (b_0 + b_1 (I\text{-}OP))] - [PROB^0 (b_0 + b_2 + b_1 I) + (1\text{-}PROB^0) (b_0 + b_1 I)], \tag{2.9}$$

where b_2 is included or excluded depending on whether $Q^1=1$ or $Q^1=0$ as defined above. Maximum OP occurs when $\Delta V = 0$. If we reduce Equation 2.9 and substitute BID for OP, the utility theoretic equation is:

$$\Delta V = b_1 BID + b_2 \Delta H_2 OSAFETY. \tag{2.10}$$

COMPARISON OF RESULTS

Comparing the Georgia and Maine results reported in Tables 2.2a, 2.2b, 2.2c, and 2.2d (*ad hoc* models) and Table 2.3 (utility theoretic model) shows that BID and $\Delta H_2 OSAFETY$ are significant in all equations. More of the household characteristics are significant in the Maine equations. Examining the estimation results indicates that omitting the subjective risk assessment variable did not result in major differences in the coefficient or option price estimates for the Georgia and Maine equations. One noticeable difference in the Maine equations is that removing the $\Delta H_2 OSAFETY$ variable caused CONCERN and PROACTIVE to become significant in all equations.

Table 2.1. Mean values for explanatory variables used in option price equations for ground water protection in Georgia and Maine case studies

Explanatory Variables	Mean (Standard Deviation)			
	State of Georgia		State of Maine	
	Protest	No Protest	Protest	No Protest
$\Delta H_2OSAFETY$	17.614 (26.285)	21.116 (26.628)	10.277 (22.477)	12.590 (21.116)
I (thousands)	44.474 (28.662)	47.314 (29.176)	31.942 (21.342)	33.345 (21.079)
CONCERN	.643 (.480)	.636 (.483)	.582 (.494)	.540 (.500)
PROACTIVE	.392 (.490)	.380 (.487)	.417 (.494)	.432 (.497)
CHILDREN PRESENT	.170 (.376)	.173 (.380)	.136 (.343)	.151 (.359)
PRIVATE WATER	.216 (.413)	.248 (.434)	.636 (.482)	.662 (.475)

The pattern of results noted above is suggestive evidence that at least in the Maine models removing $\Delta H_2OSAFETY$ may create an omitted variable bias that is reflected in the coefficients on the CONCERN and PROACTIVE variables. The correlation between $\Delta H_2OSAFETY$ and CONCERN that led to this effect, however, may also be evidence that CONCERN does not belong in the equations, i.e., it may simply be a crude measure itself of subjective risk probability. Despite these effects, the *ad hoc* specifications yielded roughly similar welfare estimates for a particular state and a protest bidder data sets (e.g., data sets with or without protest bidders). This stability occurs because the coefficient on BID is relatively stable across models for a particular state and protest bidder data set, while the effect of changes in the other variables are agglomerated in the coefficients of the remaining variables and the constant terms. As shown by the third column in Tables 2.2a and 2.2b, even dropping out all explanatory variables except for BID and $\Delta H_2OSAFETY$ does little to change the BID coefficient and welfare estimates for a particular state and protest bidder data set.

Because the variable CONCERN may be somewhat redundant, the *ad hoc* models were estimated dropping this variable. The results of these estimations

Table 2.2a. Ad hoc option price equation results for ground water protection, Georgia case study

Explanatory Variables	Models (1)		(2)		(3)	
	With Protest	No Protests	With Protest	No Protests	With Protest	No Protests
Intercept	.3343 (.273)	.0289 (.321)	.1878 (.260)	.1841 (.311)	.2436 (.170)	.1554 (.203)
BID	.0023[a] (.000778)	-.0026[a] (.000848)	.0016[b] (.000697)	-.0022[a] (.000792)	.0024[a] (.000762)	-.0028[a] (.000825)
$\Delta H_2OSAFETY$	-.0265[a] (.00499)	.020[a] (.00559)	—	—	-.0262[a] (.00485)	.0194[a] (.00540)
I (thousands)	.0006 (.00372)	-.0005 (.00426)	.0022 (.00345)	.0016 (.00406)	---	---
CONCERN	-.1974 (.232)	.2362 (.266)	-.2925 (.216)	.3339 (.255)	---	---
PROACTIVE	-.0760 (.232)	.1467 (.262)	-.1167 (.210)	.1395 (.250)	---	---
CHILDREN PRESENT	.3173 (.289)	-.3932 (.328)	.2587 (.273)	-.3473 (.319)	---	---

Explanatory Variables	Models					
	(1)		(2)		(3)	
	With Protest	No Protests	With Protest	No Protests	With Protest	No Protests
PRIVATE WATER	.0466 (.270)	-.0523 (.301)	.0215 (.245)	.0013 (.284)	—	---
N	171	121	171	121	171	121
Log Likelihood	-95.3619	-70.1835	-112.2260	-77.1909	-96.8517	-71.4281
Mean WTP (Hanemann)	$320	$228	$306	$234	$321	$226
Mean WTP (Cameron)	$86	$205	$60	$211	$90	$203

Notes:
Standard errors in parentheses.
[a] significant at the 1 percent level.
[b] significant at the 5 percent level.

Table 2.2b. Ad hoc option price equation results for ground water protection, Maine case study

Explanatory Variables	Models					
	(1)		(2)		(3)	
	With Protest	No Protests	With Protest	No Protests	With Protest	No Protests
Intercept	-1.2914 (0.314)	-1.2788[a] (0.391)	-1.2630[a] (0.308)	-1.2579[a] (0.379)	-0.4356[a] (0.166)	-0.3470[c] (0.201)
BID	-0.0025[a] (0.000752)	-0.0029[a] (0.000996)	-0.0025[a] (0.000745)	-0.0028[a] (0.000983)	-0.0026[a] (0.000724)	-0.0030[a] (0.000924)
$\Delta H_2 OSAFETY$	0.0146[a] (0.00510)	0.0181[a] (0.00662)	—	—	0.0174[a] (0.00469)	0.0229[a] (0.00598)
I (thousands)	0.0099[b] (0.00507)	0.0180[c] (0.00647)	0.0126[a] (0.00490)	0.0150[b] (0.00628)	—	—
CONCERN	0.3377 (0.221)	0.6740[a] (0.271)	0.4151[a] (0.216)	0.7820[a] (0.265)	—	—
PROACTIVE	0.4920[b] (0.210)	0.4186 (0.257)	0.4868[a] (0.206)	0.4462[c] (0.250)	—	—
CHILDREN PRESENT	-0.4068 (0.312)	-0.5506 (0.372)	0.4197 (0.309)	-0.5889 (0.366)	—	—

Explanatory Variables	Models					
	(1)		(2)		(3)	
	With Protest	No Protests	With Protest	No Protests	With Protest	No Protests
PRIVATE WATER	0.2418 (0.227)	0.0733 (0.282)	0.2883 (0.222)	0.1238 (0.274)	—	—
N	206	139	206	139	206	139
Log Likelihood	-94.5263	-64.2203	-98.6343	-68.0224	-102.7311	-72.4746
Mean WTP (Hanemann)	$94	$105	$97	$109	$100	$115
Mean WTP (Cameron)	-$131	-$51	-$115	-$55	-$101	-$20

Notes:
Standard errors in parentheses.
[a] significant at the 1 percent level
[b] significant at the 5 percent level
[c] significant at the 10 percent level

Table 2.2c. Ad hoc option price equation (without CONCERN variable) results for ground water protection, Georgia case study

Explanatory Variables	Models			
	(4)		(5)	
	With Protest	No Protests	With Protest	No Protests
Intercept	0.2271 (0.242)	0.1548 (0.287)	0.0218 (0.226)	0.3758 (0.273)
BID	0.0023[a] (0.000772)	-0.0026[a] (0.000842)	0.0016[b] (0.000691)	-0.0022[a] (0.000784)
$\Delta H_2 OSAFETY$	-0.0265[a] (0.00494)	0.0198[a] (0.00551)	—	—
I (thousands)	0.0006 (0.00370)	-0.0008 (0.00422)	-0.0020 (0.00344)	0.002 (0.00402)
CONCERN	—	—	—	—
PROACTIVE	-0.1177 (0.220)	0.1896 (0.257)	-0.1846 (0.204)	0.2016 (0.245)
CHILDREN PRESENT	0.2936 (0.287)	-0.3676 (0.257)	0.2286 (0.272)	-0.3172 (0.318)

Explanatory Variables	Models			
	(4)		(5)	
	With Protest	No Protests	With Protest	No Protests
PRIVATE WATER	0.0189 (0.266)	-0.0144 (0.327)	-0.0184 (0.242)	0.0554 (0.278)
N	171	121	171	121
Log Liklihood	-95.7245	-70.5778	-113.1425	-78.0483
Mean WTP (Hanemann)	$320	$229	$307	$234
Mean WTP (Cameron)	$88	$206	$64	$211

Notes:
Standard errors in parentheses.
[a] significant at the 1 percent level.
[b] significant at the 5 percent level.

Table 2.2d. Ad hoc option price equation (without CONCERN variable) results for ground water protection, Maine case study

Explanatory Variables	Models			
	(4)		(5)	
	With Protest	No Protests	With Protest	No Protests
Intercept	-1.1481[a] (0.295)	-1.0271[a] (0.364)	-1.0791[a] (0.287)	-0.9586[a] (0.348)
BID	-0.0024[a] (0.000746)	-0.0029[a] (0.000967)	-0.0024[a] (0.000737)	-0.0028[a] (0.000942)
$\Delta H_2OSAFETY$	0.0155[a] (0.00504)	0.0202[a] (0.00640)	—	—
I (thousands)	0.0100[b] (0.00504)	0.0128[b] (0.00636)	0.0129[a] (0.00485)	0.0167[a] (0.00611)
CONCERN	—	—	—	—
PROACTIVE	0.5235[a] (0.208)	0.4803[c] (0.251)	0.5265[a] (0.204)	0.5154[b] (0.243)

Explanatory Variables	Models			
	(4)		(5)	
	With Protest	No Protests	With Protest	No Protests
CHILDREN PRESENT	-0.3717 (0.309)	-0.4221 (0.356)	-0.3796 (0.306)	-0.4441 (0.348)
PRIVATE WATER	0.2716 (0.225)	0.1311 (0.275)	0.3303 (0.219)	0.2153 (0.264)
N	206	139	206	139
Log likelihood	-95.7113	-67.4061	-100.5121	-72.5725
Mean WTP (Hanemann)	$95	$110	$99	$116
Mean WTP (Cameron)	-$136	-$39	-$118	-$37

Notes:
Standard errors in parentheses.
[a] significant at the 1 percent level.
[b] significant at the 5 percent level.
[c] significant at the 10 percent level.

Table 2.3. Utility theoretic option price equation results for ground water protection, Georgia and Maine case studies

Explanatory Variables	Georgia		Maine	
	With Protest	No Protests	With Protest	No Protests
BID	0.0031[a]	-0.0024[a]	-0.0039[a]	-0.0041[a]
	(0.00061)	(0.000671)	(0.0005)	(0.0007)
$\Delta H_2OSAFETY$	0.0239[a]	0.0211[a]	-0.0129[a]	0.0190[a]
	(0.00457)	(0.00493)	(0.0043)	(0.0055)
N	171	121	206	139
Log Likelihood	-97.3806	-71.7217	-106.2565	-73.7904
Mean WTP (Hanemann)	$312	$221	$116	$126
Mean WTP (Cameron)	$137	$185	$34	$58

Notes:
Standard errors in parentheses.
[a] significant at the 1 percent level.
[b] significant at the 5 percent level.
[c] significant at the 10 percent level.

are reported in Tables 2.2c and 2.2d. When CONCERN is dropped the magnitude of the coefficient on PROACTIVE increases as would be expected because averting behavior would likely pick up some of the effects of a general concern over water quality. The magnitudes of the coefficients on other explanatory variables in the Maine models also increase slightly. Dropping the CONCERN variable did not result in much of a difference in mean option price estimates for a particular state and protest bidder data set.

Some interesting observations arise when comparing the estimation results across protest bidder data sets (e.g., with or without protest bidders). In the case of the state of Georgia, the signs of explanatory variable coefficients in the 'no protest bidder' models are more consistent with theoretical expectations as compared to the models that include 'protest bidders.' Because we should not expect true 'protest bidders' to necessarily behave in an economically rational manner, this result is not a major surprise. In both the Georgia and Maine cases, removing protest bidders increased the magnitude of the BID coefficient as we would expect. In the case of Maine, other differences between the models estimated with and without protest bidders appear relatively minor.

In the case of Georgia, removing protest bidders decreases welfare estimates. Conceptually, removing protest bidders is generally expected to increase willingness-to-pay welfare estimates. In the case of the state of Maine, removing protest bidders increased welfare estimates as expected.

Comparison of welfare estimate results across the *ad hoc* and utility theoretic models does not suggest major differences. However, the utility theoretic models generate what we would consider the 'best' estimates of willingness-to-pay for ground water quality in terms of theoretical expectations and empirical (e.g., 'on-the-ground') plausibility. This result reinforces the importance of practicing both the application of sound economic theory and empirical estimation techniques when estimating the value of water quality.

IMPLICATIONS AND CONCLUSIONS

The estimated option price equations revealed that subjective risk assessment is a statistically strong determinant of option price as is suggested by the theoretical water valuation model discussed in this chapter and in Chapter 1 of this book. Previous water valuation studies have not always included a risk assessment variable. The results presented in this chapter beg the question, 'Does omitting a risk assessment variable from a water quality option price equation lead to biased option price results?' Option price estimates which are biased upwards or downwards can lead to flawed water policy and management decisions. In our case study, omitting subjective risk assessment from the option price equations did not result in major changes in the significance levels of other determinants of option price. Removing protest bidders increased welfare estimates as expected in most cases. By and large, welfare estimates appeared to be most sensitive to a researcher's choice of culling of protest bidders. Because of the sensitivity of welfare estimates to research methods, water policy decisions and outcomes based on economic valuations may turn on subjective decisions that a researcher makes with respect to data collection and analysis. Using utility theoretic specifications for the option price equations rather than *ad hoc* specifications appeared to generate the 'best' overall set of welfare estimates in terms of theoretical expectations and empirical plausibility. We cannot say for certain that our utility theoretic option price equations came closest to measuring the 'true' unknown option price for ground water quality protection in the States of Georgia and Maine. When utility theoretic and *ad hoc* specifications generate different results, we have a theoretical preference for option price estimates generated by utility theoretic specifications.

NOTES

1. When differences in Equation 2.4 are calculated, we have $PROB^1(Q^1) + Q^0 - PROB^1(Q^0) - PROB^0(Q^1) - Q^0 + PROB^0(Q^0) = PROB^1(1) + 0 - PROB^1(0) - PROB^0(1) - 0 + PROB^0(0) = PROB^1 - PROB^0 = \Delta H_2OSAFETY$

REFERENCES

Bergstrom, J.C., and J.H. Dorfman (1994), 'Commodity information and willingness-to-pay for groundwater quality protection', *Review of Agricultural Economics*, **16**:413-25.

Boyle, K.J., G.L. Poe, and J.C. Bergstrom (1994), 'What do we know about groundwater values? Preliminary implications from a meta analysis of contingent valuation studies', *American Journal of Agricultural Economics*, **76**:1055-61.

Cameron, T.A. (1988), 'A new paradigm for valuing non-marketing goods using referendum data: maximum likelihood estimation by censored logistic regression', *Journal of Environmental Economics and Management*, **15**:355-79.

Edwards, S.F. (1988), 'Option prices for groundwater protection', *Journal of Environmental Economics and Management*, **15**:475-87.

Hanemann, W.M. (1984), 'Welfare evaluations in contingent valuation experiments with discrete responses,' *American Journal of Agricultural Economics*, **66**(3):332-41.

Hanley, N.D. (1989), *Problems in valuing environmental improvements resulting from agricultural policy changes: the case of nitrate pollution*, Discussion Paper in Economics 89/1, Department of Economics, University of Stirling.

Jordan, J.L. and A.H. Elnagheeb (1993), 'Willingness to pay for improvement in drinking water quality', *Water Resources Research*, **29**(2):237-452.

McClelland, G.H., W.D.Schulze, J.K.Lazo, D.M. Waldman, J.K.Doyle, S.R.Elliott, and J.R.Irwin (1992), 'Methods for measuring non-use values: a contingent valuation study of groundwater cleanup', Final Report, Office of Policy, Planning, and Evaluation, US Environmental Protection Agency, Cooperative Agreement #CR-815183.

Mitchell, R.C. and R.T. Carson (1989), *Using Surveys to Value Public Goods: The Contingent Valuation Method*, Resources for the Future, Washington, DC.

Poe, G.L. and R.C. Bishop (1993), 'An empirical evaluation of incremental conditional damages and benefits', Working Paper #wp93-13, Department of Agricultural Economics, University of Wisconsin, Madison.

Powell, F.R. (1991), 'The value of ground water protection: measurement of willingness-to-pay information, and its utilization by local government decision-makers', Unpublished dissertation, Cornell University.

Shultz, S.D. and B.E.Lindsay (1990), 'The willingness to pay for ground water protection', *Water Resources Research*, **26**(9):1869-1975.

Sun, H., J.C. Bergstrom, and J.H. Dorfman (1992), 'Estimating the benefit of groundwater contamination control', *Southern Journal of Agricultural Economics*, **24**(2):63-71.

3. Information and the Valuation of Nitrates in Ground Water, Portage County, Wisconsin

Gregory L. Poe and Richard C. Bishop

INTRODUCTION

Information is an important input in value formation and the distribution of estimated contingent values (Hoehn and Randall, 1987; Bergstrom and Stoll, 1989; Samples, Dixon and Gowen, 1986; Boyle, 1989; Bergstrom, Stoll and Randall, 1990). Although critical assessments of contingent valuation stress that information provision should be 'adequate' in order to obtain satisfactory transactions and reliable values (Fischhoff and Furby, 1988; Arrow *et al.*, 1993), very little empirical research has been devoted to establishing a minimum standard of information adequacy for contingent-valuation studies. The need for such research is particularly cogent for valuing environmental risks such as ground water contamination, as this is an unfamiliar commodity valuation exercise for most households and previous research indicates that risk perceptions are affected by new information (Viscusi and O'Connor; 1984; Smith *et al.*, 1990; Smith and Johnson, 1988).

This chapter consists of two distinct but related research efforts, both of which are drawn from a contingent-valuation study conducted in Portage County, Wisconsin. First, using nitrates in ground water as a case study and drawing on research previously presented in Poe (1993, 1998), Poe *et al.* (1998), and Poe and Bishop (1999), this chapter expands the option price framework in Chapter 1 (this book) by exploring two information-related valuation issues. In Part I of this chapter we evaluate how health risk perceptions of ground water quality and the distribution of contingent values for ground water protection are affected by varying levels of information provision provided with the survey. From this research we conclude that both *specific* information about personal exposure levels based on actual well tests and *general* information about sources of contaminants, health effects, water quality standards, and opportunities for mitigation are needed to support contingent valuation programs affecting risks.

Given a *full* information set containing both general and specific information, we also estimate a damage function across nitrate levels in Part II of this chapter. As such, we provide unique ground water valuation research that directly links contingent values to actual water quality measures experienced by individuals.

INFORMATION AND VALUES FOR GROUND WATER PROTECTION

Conceptual Framework

The conceptual framework underlying this analysis extends the model developed in Chapter 1 of this book by incorporating uncertainty and information in two ways. First, because of the stochastic nature of biological and physical transport, it is reasonable to define nitrate exposure as a random variable η. Second, the distribution of health (h) outcomes plays an important role under the option price theoretical framework. Let this uncertainty be characterized by the conditional probability density $f(h;\eta)$, and let $F(h;\eta)$ represent the associated cumulative distribution function defined over the set of possible health states A.

The distributions of anticipated exposure levels and health risks are subjective and information dependent, implying that information levels need to be explicitly identified in the survey instrument and modeling. Our analysis distinguishes between information about nitrates that is general in nature and information that is specific to a household's exposure level from its own water source. *General information* (GI) about nitrates would include possible health effects and sources of nitrates, government standards, and opportunities for mitigation. With this bundle of information, the decision maker could conceivably define health effects and optimal averting and consumption strategies for each potential level of exposure. *Specific information* (SI) about nitrate levels found in an individual's well would primarily affect the subjective distribution of nitrate exposure levels.

Distributions of nitrate exposure levels are treated here as a function of both general and specific information, i.e. $\eta = \eta(GI, SI)$, as both types of information may influence the perceived distribution of nitrates. Similarly, it is argued that the perceived distribution of health outcomes is affected by both information types, i.e. f(h|η,GI, SI). Assessment of health risk is obviously a function of general information. Building on Visusi's prospect reference theory, Poe and Bishop (1999) demonstrate that the individual transformation function between nitrate exposure and health risk is also dependent on the actual 'reference' exposure level experienced by an individual. That is, individuals with high levels of exposure tend to view all exposure levels as relatively safe, whereas individuals with low exposure levels tend to view all exposure levels as relatively unsafe. The corresponding joint conditional probability distribution of exposure and conditional health outcomes links the two distributions,

$$G(h, \eta \mid GI, SI) = f(h \mid \eta, GI, SI) \, \eta \, (GI, SI) \qquad (3.1)$$

An individual's ability to assess the exposure risk and conditional health effects underlying this conditional joint probability distribution for both target and reference risks is of fundamental import in the valuation of ground water protection programs. For this reason, much of the analysis of survey responses in this section focuses on the ability of individuals to assess the safety level of their current exposure. Hence, safety perceptions serve as a proxy for exact risk distributions implied in the equations.

It is essential to note that general and specific information will not only affect perceived risks but may directly affect arguments in the constraint and utility functions. For instance, information about the price of substitute goods could affect the optimal consumption set through the budget constraint. Information about nitrate contamination may affect preferences based on non-use motivations.[1] Incorporating these ideas, the indirect utility maximization problem can be stated as

$$\max_{X} \int_{0}^{\infty}\int_{A} V_h (I - pX, \eta; GI, SI) \, d\,G(h, \eta \mid GI, SI) \, dN \qquad (3.2)$$

where I indicates income; p is a state independent vector of prices associated with goods X (which may include averting expenditures such as bottled water); N indicates nitrate levels; and all other variables have been previously defined.[2]

In this model information components are interpreted as a signal or an observation of a random variable that affects the joint probability distribution of nitrate exposure and health risks as well as elements of the utility and constraint functions. Because information affects both the subjective utility and risk aspects of the maximization problem, isolation of the separate information effects is not possible. Defining X^0 to be the optimal vector of consumption associated with the nitrate distribution (η^0) without the program and X' to be the optimal vector of consumption corresponding to the post-program nitrate distributions (η'), state independent willingness to pay (WTP) or option price is defined implicitly by

$$\int_0^\infty \int_A V_h (I - pX^0, \eta^0; GI, SI) \, dG(h, \eta^0 \mid GI, SI) \, dN =$$

$$\int_0^\infty \int_A V_h (I - pX' - WTP, \eta'; GI, SI) \, dG(h, \eta' \mid GI, SI) \, dN$$

$$(3.3)$$

In this model, WTP is considered an *ex ante* total value that accommodates both use and non-use motivations.

Survey design
As a case study, this research focused on the very specific issue of ground water protection from nitrate contamination in rural areas of Portage County, Wisconsin, that rely on private wells. Over the decades preceding the study, Portage County had experienced rising nitrate levels with the number of private wells exceeding government standards of 10 mg/l NO_3-N. The population in this area was estimated to be 22,432 in the 1990 US Census.

In order to assess how general information about contaminants and specific information about exposure levels affect risk perceptions as well as WTP for a ground water protection program, the survey design consisted of two sequential stages. Stage 1 participants received a package in the mail that included a questionnaire and water sampling kit: they were asked to return the completed questionnaire along with a water sample that would be analyzed for nitrates by the Wisconsin State Laboratory of Hygiene. In addition, households in the Stage 1 sample were divided randomly into two groups. One-half (With-GI) of the participants were provided written general information within the questionnaire about the possible health effects of nitrates, sources of nitrate contamination, government standards for nitrates, distribution of nitrate levels in Portage County wells, and possible averting and mitigating actions (see Figure 3.1). This information packet was a composite of information taken from pamphlets available from local extension, university and other government sources — i.e., sources that are readily accessible to Portage County residents through local extension offices. The other half (No-Info) of the Stage 1 sample did not receive this information packet. In the Stage 2 survey, all Stage 1 participants who returned water samples and completed a Stage 1 questionnaire were provided with their nitrate test results for their household water supply along with general information about nitrates and a second questionnaire.

> The next section and the remainder of the survey deals specifically with <u>nitrates</u>.
> Here, we provide you with important information about nitrates in your
> groundwater. PLEASE READ THIS PAGE AND THE FOLLOWING PAGE
> CAREFULLY!

Nitrates in Groundwater

★ Nitrate (NO_3) is an inorganic chemical form of nitrogen (N) that can pollute groundwater.

★ Some nitrates in groundwater come from natural sources, but high levels are usually caused by human activities.

★ The most common sources of high nitrate levels in groundwater are septic tanks; farm, lawn and garden fertilizers; livestock holding areas; and abandoned wells.

★ Causes of contamination of any given well depend on local factors such as well location and regional factors such as geology, land use, and farming practices. For this reason, sources of high nitrate levels in individual wells vary from area to area.

★ Unless they drink water from wells from high nitrate levels, most people get more nitrates from food than from water.

Nitrates and Blue Baby Syndrome

★ For some infants, consumption of high nitrate water can reduce the ability of the blood to carry oxygen. Affected infants experience symptoms of suffocation, and they may turn a bluish-gray color. This disease is called "blue baby" syndrome.

★ Blue baby syndrome can be fatal. Infants can be protected from blue baby syndrome by using water that meets the government safety standards for nitrates.

★ This disease is only thought to affect infants less than 6 months old; older children and adults are <u>not known</u> to be affected.

Nitrates and Cancer

★ Some areas with high nitrate levels in the drinking water have unusually high rates of stomach, gastric, and lymph node cancer, although scientists have not determined whether these cancers were caused by nitrates in well water.

★ Nitrates may be converted to nitrosamines, which are chemicals that are known to cause cancer.

Government Standards for Nitrates

★ Federal and state authorities have established a safety standard of 10 milligrams per liter (mg/l) of nitrates (NO_3 as N) for municipal or other public water supplies.

★   This standard was established to protect infants from blue baby syndrome. Possible cancer risks were not considered when creating this standard.

★   If the nitrate levels of a <u>public</u> water supply exceed this standard the water has to be treated or another water source has to be found. For example, the public well in the Village of Whiting has been closed since 1979 because of high nitrate levels.

★   The federal and state standards do not apply to <u>private</u> wells serving individual homes.

Nitrates in Portage County Wells

★   About 18 percent of the private wells that have been tested in Portage County have nitrates in excess of the safety standard, compared to 10 percent of all wells in Wisconsin.

★   Many more Portage County wells meet the standard of 10 mg/l, but have nitrates that exceed natural levels. Natural levels in Wisconsin are 2 to 3 mg/l or less.

★   Nitrate levels are increasing in many Wisconsin wells.

Solutions to High Nitrates found in Drinking Water

★   Communities can avoid high nitrates in drinking water by regulating or eliminating sources of contamination, installing a community well, or by finding other sources of water.

★   Individuals can avoid high nitrates in drinking water by using one of the following options:
    <u>Well reconstruction or installation of a new well</u> can cost several hundred to several thousand dollars. However, improving your well does not guarantee low nitrate levels.
    <u>Bottled water</u> that is delivered to your home costs about $160 to $235 per person per year.
    <u>Single-tap purification systems</u> cost $525 to $700 to purchase and install, with annual maintenance costs of $20 to $40. These systems use reverse osmosis, and they remove 85 percent or more of nitrates in water.
    <u>Whole-home purification systems</u> costs $1500 or more to purchase and install, with annual maintenance costs of $50 to $100. These systems use anion exchange processes and keep nitrates to less than 6 mg/l.

★   Water softeners and simple charcoal filters do <u>not</u> remove nitrates. Also, do <u>not</u> boil water to remove nitrates. Boiling actually concentrates nitrates due to evaporation.

Figure 3.1.   Example of general information provided in stage 1 with info questionnaires, Wisconsin case study

In all, this survey design resulted in three different treatments for the analysis of information effects: the 'No-Info' group received no information in the Stage 1 questionnaire; the 'With-GI' group received general information about nitrates in the Stage 1 questionnaire; and the 'Stage 2'participants received both general and specific information about nitrates. This design allowed the evaluation of the impacts of general information on questionnaire responses by comparing the No-Info and With-GI group responses. The effect of specific information was evaluated by comparing the Stage 1 and Stage 2 responses.   The implementation of the survey followed established mail survey procedures. A total of 480 participants were randomly selected for the Stage 1 survey from a private mailing list covering areas of Portage County without publicly provided water.   After correcting for wrong addresses (n_{bad}=31), approximately 78 percent of the households returned a completed Stage 1 questionnaire and water sample. The conditional response rate to the Stage 2 survey was approximately 82 percent. Combined, the overall response rate for both stages was about 64 percent.

General Information, Learning, and Risk Perceptions: Stage 1
Difference in means tests of demographic characteristics across Stage 1 information treatments indicated that there were no significant differences in gender, age and education levels of respondents, household sizes and age distributions, memberships in environmental organizations, associations with farming, and household incomes between the No-Info and the With-GI treatments (Poe, 1993). In addition, the characteristics of wells and mitigating activities were statistically similar across information groups. On this basis, we concluded that information treatments were drawn from the same socioeconomic population. As such, observed differences in risk perceptions and contingent values across information groups can be attributed to informational rather than sampling effects.

In addition to the different information flows provided in the study, results from a prestudy indicated that Portage County households varied widely in the amount of prior information gathering with respect to nitrates in their drinking water supplies. Notably, a large proportion of pretest subjects (~60%) had tested their water previously for nitrates. Applying difference of means tests to the Stage 1 responses, it was subsequently determined that people who had previously tested their water for nitrates (With-Test) had significantly higher levels of education and income, were younger and had more family members (especially children) in the household than the people who had not previously tested their water (No-Test) (Poe, 1993). The wells of the With-Test group also tended to be newer than those of the No-Test group, and a significantly higher proportion of With-Test well owners had undertaken averting actions (e.g., using water from another well, purchasing bottled water). Based on these comparisons it was concluded that the With-Test and the No-Test groups constituted self-selected subpopulations in Portage County, and were separated in the Stage 1 analyses. As a result, four separate groups are identified in the Stage 1 analysis: No-Info, No-Test (NINT, n=76); With-GI, No-Test (WINT, n=73); No-Info , With-Test (NIWT, n=93), and With-GI, With-Test (WIWT, n=97).

Learning

A fundamental question in valuation research is whether individuals learn from information provided in valuation scenarios. In this study, the degree of learning attributed to general information provision was measured in the Stage 1 survey using a nine-point quiz on nitrate contamination. Mean quiz scores (standard deviations) for each information group are as follows: NINT = 2.57(2.09); NIWT = 3.70(2.30); WINT = 5.43(2.97); and WIWT = 6.24(2.33). Using standard two-sided difference of means tests and a significance level of 10 percent, each of the With-GI groups had significantly higher test scores than their No-Info counterparts. Prior water testing also appears to be correlated with knowledge about nitrates, as demonstrated by statistically higher scores for the With-Test groups relative to their No-Test counterparts.

Hypothetical Conditional Safety Perceptions

The ability to link perceptions of safety to different nitrate levels was addressed by the following question:

Q17.   Suppose that your well water was tested for nitrates, and that your well test indicated a nitrate level of _____ mg./l. In your opinion would you believe that this well is safe or unsafe for your household to use as the primary source of drinking water? (CIRCLE ONE NUMBER)

Nitrate levels 2, 4, 6, 8, 10, 12, 15, 20, 30, and 40 mg/l were randomly assigned to respondents. Categorical response options included 'Definitely Safe,' 'Probably Safe,' 'Not Very Safe,' 'Definitely Not Safe' and 'Don't Know.' For those who did not select the 'Don't Know' response option, average response patterns follow expected patterns that reflect the government health standard of 10 mg/l NO_3 - N. With increasing nitrate levels, the mass of the distribution shifted from the 'Definitely safe' and the 'Probably safe' categories to 'Not very safe' and 'Definitely not safe.'

Of greater interest in this analysis is the magnitude of 'Don't Know' responses to safety questions, which provide an indicator of respondent inability to assess the relative safe level of different nitrate levels, and hence act as an indicator of respondent uncertainty in conditional health risk perceptions. As indicated in the first column of Table 3.1, the proportion of 'Don't Know' responses to Q17 fell from 0.46 to 0.19 when general information was provided.

Thus it appears that assimilation of general information does engender greater ability to assess the safety of different exposure levels. A similar improvement in the ability to assess conditional health risks was noted for the impact of prior nitrate tests. On average, the proportion of *'Don't Know'* responses fell from 0.45 to 0.22 between the No-Test and the With-Test groups. Thus, previous experience with nitrate testing appears to be associated with the gathering and retention of general as well as specific information.

Current Exposure Levels
The respondents' ability to assess their current levels of nitrates in their household wells was evaluated with the following question:

Q23.   Federal and state authorities have established safety standards for concentration of nitrates in the ground water. Based on what you have heard and read, or any previous water tests that you may have taken, do you think that your well water has...(CIRCLE ONE NUMBER)

Categorical response options ranged from *'Much less nitrates than the safety standard (less than ½)'* to *'Much more nitrates than the safety standard (more than double).'* Again, a *'Don't Know'* option was included. As demonstrated in the second column of Table 3.1, general information alone did not have a significant effect on the number of *'Don't Know'* responses. A significant reduction was, however, associated with prior nitrate testing. Most notably, the high proportion of *'Don't Know'* responses in the No-Test group (~53%) reflects the high degree of uncertainty about exposures for that group. In the context of Equation 3.1, this suggests a poorly defined distribution of perceived exposure levels.

Personal Safety Levels
Further evidence of general information and prior testing effects on uncertainty in the joint conditional probability distribution expressed in Equation 3.1 are found in the responses to the following questions.

*Q24.   **In your opinion** are the nitrate levels found in your well safe for **adults** and **children older than 6 months** to use as their primary source of drinking and cooking water?*

*Q25.   **In your opinion** are the nitrate levels found in your well safe for **infants less than 6 months old** to use as their primary source of drinking and cooking water?*

Table 3.1. Comparisons of 'don't know' responses to selected stage 1
Questions, Wisconsin case study[a]

Group	Safety of Hypothetical Nitrate Levels Q17	Level of Nitrates in Well Q23	Adult Safety of Nitrate Levels in Well Q24	Infant Safety of Nitrate Levels in Well Q25
No-Info	0.46	0.31	0.23	0.29
With-GI	0.19	0.30	0.26	0.31
No-Test	0.45	0.53	0.42	0.50
With-Test	0.22	0.13	0.10	0.14
NINT	0.63	0.55	0.47	0.51
NIWT	0.33	0.12	0.07	0.10
WINT	0.29	0.51	0.43	0.49
WIWT	0.11	0.14	0.14	0.17

Groups Compared		Difference of Proportions Test (t values)			
No-Info	With-GI	8.25^b	0.32	-0.73	-0.55
No-Test	With-Test	4.32^b	10.82^c	9.13^b	9.68^b
NINT	WINT	6.43^b	0.91	1.49	0.60
NIWT	WIWT	4.10^b	-0.45	-2.44^a	-2.01^c
NINT	NIWT	5.63^b	11.36^b	13.63^b	11.98^b
WINT	WIWT	10.84^b	10.01^b	9.71^b	9.37^b

Notes
[a] Response Option to Question 23 was actually 'I have no idea' rather than 'Don't know.'
[b] t-test values significantly different at 1%.
[c] t-test values significantly different at 5%.

Each question employed the response format presented in Q17 above. As demonstrated in the last two columns of Table 3.1, the proportion of *'Don't Know'* responses regarding the safety of their personal water was not significantly reduced by general information. In fact, when evaluating general information effects within the With-Test group, a significantly larger proportion of *'Don't Know'* responses to safety perceptions for adults and infants was observed for the group that received general information about nitrates. This latter result provides an indication that general information may induce some uncertainty and anxiety about personal exposure levels. In contrast, ability to assess exposure levels is apparently improved by prior testing, as demonstrated by the significant decline in the proportion of *'Don't Know'* responses between the No-Test and With-Test groups and subgroups.

Future Exposure Levels
In addition to current exposure levels, individuals were asked to assess the likelihood of future exposure with the question:

Q26a.   **Without**... *a groundwater protection program, do you expect the nitrate levels in your own well to exceed the government standards . . . for nitrates during* **the next five years***?*

Responses to this question were categorical with probabilistic interpretations ranging from *'No, Definitely Not'* to *'Yes, Definitely (100 percent chance).'* In order to force a response, a *'Don't Know'* option was not included for this question. With respect to Equation 3.1, this framing of the question corresponds with defining probabilities in terms of exceeding the government health advisory level or standard.

In all cases, a bell shaped curve centered on *'Maybe (50 percent chance)'* was observed in the Stage 1 analysis (see Figure 3.2), a response distribution characteristic of uncertainty about future exposures. A chi-squared test of independence using contingency tables indicated that the With-GI and No-Info treatments were not independent ($\chi^2 = 1.24 < \chi^2_{4,.10} = 7.78$), and that the With-Test and No-Test response functions were also not independent ($\chi^2 = 3.25$). In this manner, neither general information nor prior testing were found to strongly affect assessments of the likelihood of future exposure. As such, the aggregated Stage 1 distribution is provided in Figure 3.2.

Specific Information and Risk Updating: Stage 2
As indicated, individuals received nitrate test results and general information along with the Stage 2 questionnaire. About 16 percent of the wells tested exceeded the government standard of 10 mg/l for nitrates and about 60 percent had nitrate levels of less than 5 mg/l, closely mirroring data from previous water testing programs in the region (Portage County Groundwater Plan,

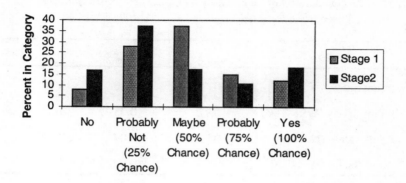

*Figure 3.2.   Stage 1 and stage 2 distributions of expectations that
Nitrate levels will exceed government standards in the
Next five years, Wisconsin case study*

1987).   A graphical depiction of their nitrate level relative to natural
background levels and the government standard was included on the inside
front cover of the Stage 2 questionnaire, and as a result participants were not
asked to estimate their current levels of exposure in the Stage 2 survey. As
noted above, all participants in the Stage 2 survey received the same full
information set, and separate Stage 1 information treatments were not isolated
in the Stage 2 analysis of risk perceptions.   Because of differences in socioeconomic characteristics, distinction between the With-Test and the No-Test
group was maintained in the Stage 2 analysis unless such a distinction was not
supported by statistical analyses. The remainder of this section examines Stage
2 responses for select questions.

Personal Safety Levels
The two safety questions for adults (Q24) and children (Q25) were repeated in
order to compare respondents' ability to provide an assessment of conditional
safety levels. This assessment corresponds with the probability distribution of
health outcomes identified in Equation 3.1. Again, the proportions of *'Don't
Know'* responses served as an indicator of respondent uncertainty about health
outcomes. The Stage 1 and Stage 2 proportion of *'Don't Know'* responses are
presented in Table 3.2 for the subsample of respondents who completed both
stages of the survey.   As demonstrated by the comparison of columns, the
proportion of *'Don't Know'* responses was reduced for all groups and safety
questions. Of these differences,
only the proportion of *'Don't Know'* responses to the adult safety question for
the With-Test group was not significantly lower in the Stage 2 survey.   The
lack of significance for this group may indicate that adult safety was conveyed
in prior testing.

Table 3.2. Comparison of 'don't know' responses for safety questions[a], Wisconsin case study

	Stage 1	Stage 2	t-Value
Infant Safety (No- Test)	0.42	0.10	10.18[b]
Infant Safety (With-Test)	0.12	0.05	4.07[b]
Adult Safety (No-Test)	0.33	0.09	7.70[b]
Adult Safety (With-Test)	0.04	0.02	1.63

Notes
[a] Only those who responded to Stage 2 questionnaire are included.
[b] t-test values significantly different at 1%.

Future Exposure Levels
As part of the contingent valuation exercise, individuals were again asked to assess their likelihood of exceeding government standards for nitrates during the next 5 years. A chi-squared contingency table analysis indicated that the Stage 1 and Stage 2 responses are statistically independent ($\chi^2 = 40.09 > \chi^2_{4,.10} = 7.78$), suggesting that updating has occurred based on the well test results. Notably, as demonstrated in Figure 3.1, a comparison of the Stage 1 and Stage 2 distributions of future exposure expectations indicates that expectations of future contamination shifted from a relatively bell-shaped distribution in Stage 1 to a bimodal distribution in Stage 2 with peaks at '*Yes, Definitely (100 percent chance)*' and '*Probably Not (25 percent chance)*.' These patterns reflect the actual distribution of nitrate test results noted above.

In addition to shifts in the sample distribution, analysis of individual risk updating within the No-Test and With-Test groups was conducted (see Poe *et al.*, 1998). In this analysis, it was found that individuals place weight on both their prior assessments and the new information provided in the water test, and that updating of risk perceptions is systematically related to nitrate levels. That is, individuals with high nitrate levels adjust towards higher risk perception levels while individuals with low nitrate levels tend to adjust their risk perceptions down. However, consistent with greater uncertainty in exposure in the Stage 1 responses, the No-Test group places greater weight on the new information contained in the nitrate test than the With-Test group.

Information and Contingent Values
A dichotomous choice contingent valuation question was employed that consisted of several parts. Participants were first provided with information about how taxpayers, individuals, and farmers pay for ground water via

government monitoring and protection programs, higher prices for goods, restrictions on agricultural practices, lower profits, and fertilizer fees. They were then asked to consider the reference and target conditions for the following ground water protection program:

* **With** the groundwater protection program, nitrate levels in all Portage County wells will **definitely** be kept below the government health standard (of 10 mg/l). In some areas this may be difficult, but suppose that it would be possible.

* **Without** the groundwater protection program, present trends in nitrate levels in Portage County will continue and the number of wells with nitrate levels higher than the government standard will increase in Portage County in the next five years.

where the statement '(of 10 mg/l)' was only included in the Stage 2 questionnaire. As discussed previously (in Q26a), individuals were then requested to provide their expectation of the likelihood that their own wells would exceed government standards for nitrates during the next five years (i.e., Pr NO$_3$-N>10), which was followed by the dichotomous choice question:

Q26b   Would you vote for the groundwater program described above if the total **annual** cost to your household (in increased taxes, lower profits, higher costs, and higher prices) were $_____ each **year** beginning now and for as long as you live in Portage County?

A randomly selected dollar value (Bid) was inscribed in each questionnaire. Mailings were conducted sequentially so as to update the bids as suggested by Kanninen (1993). Bid values for the first wave of the Stage 1 survey (225 surveys) were based on estimated logit functions from Sun's (1990) analysis, with bid values ranging from $1 to $2,500. Bid values for subsequent waves (255 surveys) were revised downward based on preliminary responses to the first wave of the survey. Note that the term waves used here refers to separate sub-samples rather than repeated sampling of the same group. The range in Stage 2 was bound between $1 and $1,000. To avoid self-selection and other complicating factors in drawing comparisons across groups, analysis is limited here to those respondents who received a bid of $1,000 or less in the Stage 1 questionnaire.

A logistic distribution was used to estimate the WTP response function:

$$Pr(Yes) = (1 + e^{-(\alpha + \beta_1 (PrNO_3 - N > 10) + \beta_2 BID)})^{-1} \tag{3.4}$$

where α, β_1 and β_2 are coefficients to be estimated and variable definitions are provided in Table 3.3. Because of small sample size for individual information and prior water testing cells, the data were combined into With-Test and No-Test groups on the basis of the previous conclusion that these groups represent distinct subpopulations. In addition, differences in information provision are accounted for within each test group by binary variables that shift the constant (General Information) and the coefficient on dichotomous choice bid values (General Information * Bid).

Table 3.3. Descriptive statistics, information effects, Wisconsin case study

Variable		No-test (n=78)	With-test (n=116)	Sign Expectation
Pr(NO₃-N> 10 mg/l) Stage 1	Probabilistic categorical variable: 0, 0.25, 0.50, 0.75, and 1.00 probability of exceeding standards.	0.47 (0.28)	0.47 (0.28)	+
Pr(NO₃-N> 10 mg/l) Stage 2	Probabilistic categorical variable: 0, 0.25, 0.50, 0.75, and 1.00 probability of exceeding standards.	0.38 (0.34)	0.46 (0.33)	+
General Information	General information provided in Stage 1 = 1.	0.45 (0.50)	0.48 (0.50)	?
Stage 1 Bid	Dichotomous Choice Dollar Value.	273.84 (317.42)	290.01 (292.12)	–
Stage 2 Bid	Dichotomous Choice Dollar Value.	240.72 (262.25)	256.48 (268.14)	–

Descriptive statistics and estimated results are presented in Table 3.3 and Table 3.4, respectively. In the Stage 1 analysis of the With-Test group, 'constant' or 'slope' information effects were not found to be individually or jointly significant ($\chi^2 = 1.32 < 4.61 = \chi^2{}_{0.10,2}$), suggesting a limited impact of general information on people who had previously tested their wells. As a result, these coefficients are not reported in Table 3.3. In contrast, the information effects on the No-Test group were individually and jointly significant ($\chi^2 = 6.35 > 4.61 = \chi^2{}_{0.10,2}$). These results further suggest that the No-Test group is more greatly influenced by information. Interestingly the coefficient on ($Pr(NO_3\text{-}N) > 10mg/l$) is not significant in either of the Stage 1 regressions. This may be due, in part, to the small sample sizes, but also suggests that perceptions of exposure, when specific information is not provided, do not exert a strong influence on WTP.

In the Stage 2 analysis, any general information effects associated with the Stage 1 variations did not have a significant effect in either group (No-Test χ^2 = 2.21 < 4.61= $\chi^2{}_{0.10,2}$, With-Test χ^2 = 3.73). Further, an independence test across the No-Test and the With-Test groups was not significant ($\chi2 = 2.48 < 4.61 = \chi^2{}_{0.10,2}$). As a result, the Stage 2 results are pooled in Table 3.4. In contrast to the Stage 1 regression, the estimated coefficient on $Pr(NO_3\text{-}N) > 10$ mg/l is highly significant.

General Information, Specific Information, and Mean WTP
The information effects for the Stage 1 response function suggest that general information flattens out the response function across bid values for the No-Test group. The shift in WTP is reflected in the corresponding distributions of mean WTP created using a parametric bootstrap approach discussed in Park, Loomis, and Creel (1991) and integration of the estimated logistic function across positive WTP values[3]. As presented in Table 3.5, general information appears to increase the mean WTP and reduces the precision of that estimate for the No-Test group. Two causes for increased dispersion associated with general information provision alone are conjectured for the Stage 1 No-Test group. The first is that in assimilating general information, households may selectively focus on, or react to, different facets of information that are pertinent to their life situation or preferences. For example, a household with small children might react quite differently to information about blue baby syndrome than a household of retirees. In contrast to homogeneous commodities for which information is expected to increase the uniformity of the service and reduce the variance of WTP (Boyle, 1989; Bergstrom, Stoll and Randall, 1990), such heterogeneity in the population and exposure levels would be expected to widen the distribution of WTP and decrease the precision of the mean value.

Second, the relatively large spread of WTP and mean WTP for the WINT group might be attributed to an informational imbalance. Previous research has

Table 3.4. Logistic Estimation results for stage 1 and stage 2

Variable	Stage 1		Stage 2
	No-Test (s.e.)	With-Test (s.e.)	Joint (s.e.)
Constant	0.5618 (0.5992)	-0.3261 (0.4065)	-0.6345 (0.3016)[b]
Pr(NO3-N) > 10 mg/l	1.0212 (0.9361)	1.1648 (0.8138)	2.6755 (0.5426)[a]
General Information	-1.475 (0.6709)[b]		
General Information * Bid [c]	0.0050 (0.0021)[b]		
Bid	-0.0062 (0.0020)[a]	-0.0039 (0.0009)[a]	-0.0034 (0.0008)[a]
n	78	116	194
Likelihood Ratio χ^2	19.34[a]	24.91[a]	54.44[a]
Percent Correctly Predicted	72	67	74

Notes
[a] 1 percent significance levels.
[b] 5 percent significance levels.
[c] 10 percent significance levels.
Standard errors in parentheses.

suggested that too much information may create confusion about the value placed on a resource or commodity (Bergstrom and Stoll, 1989; Grether and Wilde, 1983). In this study, possible confusion associated with general information could instead be attributed to the fact that there was not enough information presented in the general information packet. Individuals were presented with an abundance of information about nitrate related health risks and possible methods of avoiding exposure, but remained uncertain about their actual exposure levels. With such uncertainty about reference exposure and safety levels, individuals may become confused about the values that they place on ground water protection and may need more information to make a satisfactory transaction. In this manner, information overload, which is an absolute concept, does not seem to be a problem. Rather, the wide dispersion of values may be attributed to an informational imbalance.

Table 3.5. Bootstrap estimates of mean WTP, Wisconsin case study

	Row	Lower Bound, 90% CI	Mean at Parameters	Upper Bound, 90% CI.	Significantly Different from Row at 10% level
Stage 1, NINT	a	136.35	213.09	464.47	b
Stage 1, WINT	b	227.14	556.40	4,744.97	a
Stage 1, With-Test	c	242.15	306.87	430.99	
Stage 2, Joint	d	226.40	285.19	394.64	

Using a significance level of $\alpha=0.10$ and the convolutions technique presented in Poe *et al.* (1994), the mean WTP for the WINT Stage 1 group is significantly different from the mean WTP for the NINT Stage 1 group. All other comparisons in Table 3.5 are not significantly different.

Discussion of Information Effects

The above analyses suggest that information presented in a contingent valuation study does affect individual ability to assess general safety associated with ground water (as measured by changes in '*Don't Know*' responses), but does not, by itself, improve the ability of individuals to assess their actual exposure and safety. Specific information provided about nitrates in individual wells (and prior water testing) does apparently reduce uncertainty about exposure levels and diminish the impact of general information effects. Notably, individuals update their exposure perceptions when provided specific well information from nitrate testing, and there is some evidence that general information provision does affect WTP, but only in the absence of any type of prior testing information. This condition of not having prior specific information is likely to typify the population consuming ground water in most parts of the world.

Taken together, these observations question the standard contingent valuation approach that has been used in the past to value ground water in which participants are provided with general information about contaminants but given little specific indication of the actual quality of their own wells.

Rather, exposure or safety levels have been frequently left to subjective, typically uninformed, perceptions provided by the respondent. Based on the above analyses, one must ask under these conditions 'Do respondents have adequate information to make reasonable and informed willingness to pay decisions about their own wells that reflect their own best interests?' Our research suggests that they do not. Moreover, our results suggest that providing general information alone may inflate WTP estimates.

ESTIMATING A DAMAGE FUNCTION[4]

We now explore the second research question of estimating a damage function across nitrate levels. Beyond the reliability of value estimates for specific ground water conditions, there is a need to design research so as to provide critical information to ground water managers and policy makers. A recent National Research Council panel (1997) notes that policy makers and managers require information about how economic values will be affected by a decision that changes levels of contamination, reflecting, in part, the theoretical requisites for identifying optimal ground water pollution policies, which rest on the notion of damage functions across nitrate exposure levels (e.g., Conrad and Olson, 1992). Conceptually, damage functions also provide the necessary information for evaluating the welfare effects of alternative land use practices on the distributions of pollutants (e.g., Wu and Babcock, 1995).

Clearly, for management purposes a damage function approach linking actual exposures to values would be useful for linking social benefits to the control of pollutants. Such a damage function also offers the possibility of improved benefit transfers by primarily relying on objective data that might be obtained from previous water quality research in the target area.

In the full information setting a damage function could be obtained by analyzing contingent valuation responses according to:

$$Pr(Yes) = (1 + e^{-(\alpha + \beta_1 (N^c) + \beta_2 BID)})^{-1} \qquad (3.5)$$

where N^C indicates nitrate levels raised to a power (c) so as to capture potential convexities. If $c>1$ ($c<1$) then the estimated damage function will be convex (concave) where c is estimated here using a grid search. This estimation may be made conditional on socio-demographic variables of the type that could be linked to census data. Here we include (with expected signs): the age (-) and gender (?) of the respondent; presence of children less than 4 years of age in the household (+); involvement in farming (-); education level (+); and household income (+). Definitions of these variables are provided in Table 3.6, along with sample means.

*Table 3.6.   Description of the covariates for the econometric analysis,
            Wisconsin case study*

Variable	Description	Mean[a] (S.D.)	Sign Expectation
OWNAGE	Categorical Variable for Years of Age: 1= less than 18; 2 = 18 to 44; 3=45 to 64; 4 = 65 or older.	2.67 (2.76)	-
DGENDER	Binary variable for gender of respondent: 0= male; 1= female.	0.38 (0.48)	?
DAGE<4	Binary variable for young children < 4 years of age in household: 0=no; 1=yes.	0.18 (0.39)	+
DFARM	Binary variable for involvement in farming: 0=no; 1= yes.	0.20 (0.40)	-
DCGRAD	Binary variable for college grad: 0=no; 1=yes.	0.25 (0.43)	+
INCOME	Categorical variable for total household income before taxes: 1= < \$10,000; 2=\$10,000 to \$19,999; 3=\$20,000 to 29,999...10=\$90,000 to 100,000; 11= >\$100,000.	4.07 (2.07)	+
$Pr(NO_3\text{-}N>$ 10 mg/l)	Probabilistic categorical variable: 0, 0.25, 0.50, 0.75, and 1.00 probability of exceeding standards.	0.45 (0.35)	+
N	Nitrate Level (NO_3-N) in mg/l, continuous from 0.15 mg/l.	6.76 (6.63)	+
Bid	Dichotomous choice dollar value.	271.72 (276.76)	+

Note
[a]185 observations.

Using the complete Stage 2 data set (i.e., without restricting observations to those participants with Stage 1 dichotomous choice bids less than $1000), the results of the estimation process are summarized in Table 3.7. The first column of this table defines the coefficients to be estimated. Columns (2) to (4) report coefficients and estimated summary statistics from maximum likelihood estimates corresponding to Equation 3.4. Different columns in this set correspond to different specifications of the nitrate and socioeconomic variables. In the first specification, the $Pr(NO_3\text{-}N > 10 \text{ mg/l})$ and bid are the only variables. The second specification expands the definition to include all the socioeconomic variables except income. The third specification also includes income as a covariate at the cost of losing about 10 percent of the observations due to item non-response. The final three columns of Table 3.7 report the estimated demand function defined by Equation 3.5 for the same sequence of covariates, where N^C replaces $PR(NO_3 - N > 10 \text{ mg/l})$.

Within each specification of the nitrate variable, the three models exhibit similar trends. Coefficients on the nitrate variables are highly significant, with appropriate signs in all specifications. Of the equations where income (I) is not included as a covariate, the coefficients on OWNAGE and DCGRAD are negative and positive respectively, as expected. The remaining coefficients are not significant. When income (I) is included, all the coefficients for the non-nitrate and non-dollars covariates become insignificant. This suggests that estimation of a WTP function will be dominated by the level of exposure and income. Should this result be supported by future research, transfers of these damage functions to other sites might be accomplished by relatively simple models of income and exposure.

From the perspective of local ground water management, it is useful policy to have WTP estimated as a function of nitrate levels. Such a direct estimate is provided in the last three columns of Table 3.7. In this analysis, the coefficient on N^C indicates an increasing but concave function of nitrates by the finding that C<1. Given the grid search approach adopted here, direct statistical tests of concavity are not performed. Yet, support for this conclusion is found by bootstrapping the data set and identifying an optimal C for each bootstrap sample. Adopting this approach, 85 of 100 bootstrap estimations provided values of less than 1.

Table 3.8 provides the associated WTP values for selected subjective probabilities of future exposure and selected nitrate exposure levels. For the subjective probability model, estimated WTP rises from about $150 for households with a zero subjective probability of exceeding standards to a maximum of $564 when the subjective probability of exceeding standards is one. The last two columns of Table 3.8 provide values for select nitrate levels ranging from 2 mg/l, the highest natural level of nitrates, to 40 mg/l. Interestingly, the WTP values from the two models converge at the upper end of the subjective probability and the nitrate exposure models.

Figure 3.3 graphically depicts the continuous damage function based on the simple model in the column (5) of Table 3.7. This direct nitrate exposure model provides a concave function that levels off at higher reference exposure levels, a result that is consistent with opportunities for substitutes such as water treatment or bottled water (part of the information packet provided with the Stage 2 survey). For comparison, a damage function is derived from the subjective probability model by averaging expectations of exceeding standards across reasonable ranges of nitrate levels. In contrast to the concave damage function, the estimated damages in this approach rise gradually across low levels of NO_3-N contamination, jump sharply as reference exposures cross 10 mg/l, and then begin to level off as the expectations of exceeding 10 mg/l approach 100 percent. The resulting damage mapping suggests an 'S' shaped function of damages, wherein a convex function corresponding to standard value of life hypothesis occurs across lower values but the WTP values are eventually truncated from above. In addition, the small rise in values observed in the 2-3 mg/l range correspond with the fact that 2 mg/l is the highest natural level of nitrates in ground water and the observation that households in the 2-3 mg/l range had relatively high subjective probabilities. Combined, these findings suggest that the elevated risk perceptions reflect an alarmist reaction to being near the threshold of natural and human-caused contaminant levels.

IMPLICATIONS AND CONCLUSIONS

The objective of this chapter is to suggest that future ground water valuation research adopt a new valuation paradigm that WTP estimates be based on respondents have specific information about their actual exposure levels. Arguments in support of such a proposal center on the credibility of individual WTP responses along with the need to provide water managers, land use managers, and policy makers with valuation data that can be linked to decision making about water contamination levels.

Toward this objective, we demonstrate that information effects do occur in risk and exposure perceptions and WTP, and provide the first CV survey of ground water nitrate contamination to be based on actual exposure levels experienced by respondents. Key findings of this research are that a full information approach that includes both general and specific information about health exposures and risk apparently helps respondents define their reference and target risks, and that damages appear to be a concave function of nitrates and are bounded from above. This latter result is consistent with opportunities for substitution such as water treatment and bottled water.

In recommending that a fully informed approach should underlie future water valuation research, we recognize that testing water quality may be expensive, perhaps prohibitively so in some situations. In cases where cost prevents

Table 3.7. *Full information subjective probability of exceeding standards and nitrate exposure models, Wisconsin case study*

Variable	Subjective Probability Model			Nitrate Exposure Model		
	(2)	(3)	(4)	(5)	(6)	(7)
Constant	-0.3617 (0.2889)	0.6296 (0.8057)	-1.3293 (1.0567)	-0.4739 (0.5117)	-0.8281 (0.8819)	-0.8809 (1.1298)
OWNAGE		-0.4400 (0.2453)[c]	-0.1013 (0.2797)		-0.5138 (0.2290)[b]	-0.1998 (0.2588)
DGENDER		-0.1036 (0.3415)	0.2173 (0.3914)		-0.0499 (0.3312)	0.1837 (0.3720)
DAGE<4		-0.1998 (0.4519)	-0.0417 (0.4963)		0.1548 (0.441)	0.0365 (0.4775)
DFARM		0.2836 (0.4087)	0.5482 (0.4675)		0.2135 (0.3975)	0.4986 (0.4510)
DCGRAD		1.1141 (0.3912)[a]	0.4633 (0.4772)		1.0230 (0.3742)[a]	0.4650 (0.4476)
INCOME			0.2735 (0.1067)[a]			0.2374 (0.1005)[b]

Variable	Subjective Probability Model			Nitrate Exposure Model		
	(2)	(3)	(4)	(5)	(6)	(7)
Prob (NO$_3$-N>10)	2.1855 (0.4929)[a]	2.1153 (0.5105)[a]	2.4713 (0.5914)[a]			
C				0.3520	0.3530	0.3460
N^C				0.5842 (0.2629)[b]	0.5107 (0.2785)[c]	0.5581 (0.3168)[c]
Bid	-0.0035 (0.0007)[a]	-0.0038 (0.0007)[a]	-0.0047 (0.0009)[a]	-0.0032 (0.0007)[a]	0.0035 (0.0007)[a]	-0.0043 (0.0008)[a]
Obs.	210	210	185	210	210	185
Likelihood Ratio χ^2	53.08[a]	65.06[a]	72.96[a]	36.12[a]	49.42[a]	55.67[a]
Perc. Pred.	77	74	78	69	73	72

Notes
[a]1 percent significance level; [b]5 percent significance level; [c]10 percent significance level. Standard errors in parentheses.

Table 3.8. WTP values for selected subjective probability and nitrate
Exposure values, Wisconsin case study

Subjective Probability Model		Nitrate Exposure Model	
Prob (NO$_3$-N) > 10 mg/l	Estimated WTP ($)	NO$_3$ - N (mg/l)	Estimated WTP ($)
0.00	150.98	2	259.45
0.25	225.61	5	312.30
0.50	321.15	10	371.05
0.75	435.25	20	453.60
1.00	563.85	40	569.29

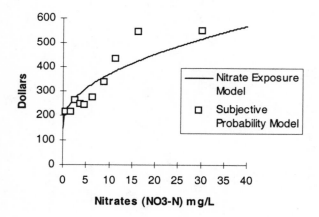

Figure 3.3. WTP as a function of nitrate levels: subjective probability and
nitrate exposure models, Wisconsin case study

individual testing of wells, researchers may turn to alternative approaches
relying more on subjective safety information such as discussed in Chapters 2
and 4 of this book or on aggregate, average information such as that used in
Chapter 5. Researchers, policy makers, and funding agencies should, however,
recognize that values based on general information may provide biased value
estimates. Further, there may be secondary off-site benefits of using objective

instruments in the estimation process. Given the high cost of conducting original CV research and eliciting subjective perceptions, damage functions based on objective data that is widely available may enhance the possibility of transferring these values to other sites.

NOTES

1. McClelland *et al.* (1992) provide an interesting two period model that accounts for these motivations. In the current analysis it is postulated that non-use motivation may enter into the valuation function, but the exact linkages are not specified.
2. A more complete model might include severity effects as measured by the costs of illness. This aspect may be important, but is ignored here. See Berger *et al.* (1987), Shogren and Crocker (1991), Crocker, Forster and Shogren (1991), and Quiggen (1992)for a discussion of this issue.
3. The truncation point for numerical integration was set at $6,000 based on numerical evaluation of the stability of mean and median values of the logistic distribution. See Poe (1993) pp. 150-52 for further discussion.
4. This section and the conclusion closely follows Poe, 1998. However, the focus here is on the mean WTP derived from integrating over the positive dollar values in the estimated logit equation rather than median WTP as described in Cameron (1988, 1992).

REFERENCES

Arrow, K., R. Solow, P. R. Portney, E.E. Leamer, R. Radner, and H. Schuman (1993), *Natural Resource Damage Assessments Under the Oil Pollution Act of 1990*, National Oceanic and Atmospheric Administration Federal Register, Vol. **58**, No. 10.

Berger, M. C., G. C. Blomquist, D. Kenkel, and G. S. Tolley (1987), 'Valuing changes in health risks: a comparison of alternative measures,' *Southern Economics Journal*, **53**: 967-84.

Bergstrom, J. C., and J. R. Stoll (1989), 'Application of experimental economics concepts and precepts to CVM field survey procedures,' *Western Journal of Agricultural Economics*, **14**:98-109.

Bergstrom, J. C., J. R. Stoll and A. Randall (1990), 'The impact of information on environmental valuation decisions,' *American Journal of Agricultural Economics*, **72**:614-21.

Boyle, K. J. (1989), 'Commodity specification and the framing of contingent-valuation questions,' *Land Economics*, **65**:57-63.

Cameron, T. A. (1988), 'A new paradigm for valuing non-market goods using referendum data: maximum likelihood estimation by censored logistic regression,' *Journal of Environmental Economics and Management*, **15**, 355-79.

Cameron, T. A. (1992), 'Interval estimates of non-market resource values from referendum contingent valuation surveys,' *Land Economics*, **67**(4): 413-21.

Conrad, J. M. and L. J. Olson (1992), 'The economics of a stock pollutant,' *Environmental and Resource Economics*, **2**: 245-58.

Crocker, T. D., B. A. Forster, and J. F. Shogren (1991), 'Valuing potential groundwater protection benefits,' *Water Resources Research*, **27**:1-6.

Fischhoff, B., and L. Furby (1988), 'Measuring values: a conceptual framework for interpreting transactions with special reference to contingent valuation of visibility,' *Journal of Risk and Uncertainty*, **1**:147-84.

Grether, D.M. and L.L. Wilde, (1983), 'Consumer choice and information: new experimental evidence,' *Information Economics and Policy* **1**:115-44.

Hoehn, J. P., and A. Randall (1987), 'A satisfactory benefit-cost indicator from contingent valuation,' *Journal of Environmental Economics and Management*, **14**:226-47.

Kanninen, B. J. (1993), 'Design of sequential experiments for contingent valuation studies,' *Journal of Environmental Economics and Management*, **25**:S-1-S-11.

McClelland, G.H., W. D. Schulze, J. K. Lazo, D. M. Waldman, J. K. Doyle, S. R. Elliott, and J. R. Irwin (1992), *Methods for Measuring Non-Use Values: A Contingent Valuation Study of Groundwater Cleanup*, Draft, US Environmental Protection Agency, Washington, DC.

National Research Council (1997), *Valuing Ground Water: Economic Concepts and Approaches*, National Academy Press, Washington, D. C.

Park, T., J. B. Loomis, and M. Creel (1991), 'Confidence intervals for evaluating benefits estimates from dichotomous choice contingent valuation studies,' *Land Economics*, **67**(1):64-73.

Poe, G. L. (1993), 'Information, risk perceptions and contingent values: the case of nitrates in groundwater,' Ph.D. dissertation, University of Wisconsin-Madison.

Poe, G. L. (1998), 'Valuation of groundwater quality using a contingent valuation-damage function approach,' *Water Resources Research*, **34**(12): 3627-33.

Poe, G. L., and R. C. Bishop (1999), 'Valuing the incremental benefits of groundwater protection when exposure levels are known,' *Environmental and Resource Economics*, **13**(3): 347-73.

Poe, G. L., H. M. van Es, T. P VandenBerg, and R. C. Bishop (1998), 'Do households update their health risk and exposure perceptions with water testing?,' *Journal of Soil and Water Conservation*, **53**(4):320-5.

Poe, G. L., E. K. Severance-Lossin, and M. P. Welsh (1994), 'Measuring the difference (x-y) of simulated distributions: a convolutions approach,' *American Journal of Agricultural Economics* **76**(4): 904-15.

Portage County Groundwater Plan (1987), Vol. 1., Portage County, Wisconsin.

Quiggen, J. (1992), 'Risk, self protection and ex ante economic value - some positive results,' *Journal of Environmental Economics and Management*, **23**:40-53.

Samples, K. C., J. A. Dixon, and M. M. Gowen (1986), 'Information disclosure and endangered species valuation,' *Land Economics*, **62**:307-12.

Shogren, J. F., and T. C. Crocker (1991), 'Risk, self-protection and ex ante economic value,' *Journal of Environmental Economics and Management*, **20**:1-15.

Smith, V. K., and F. R. Johnson (1988), 'How do risk perceptions respond to information? The case of radon,' *The Review of Economics and Statistics*, **70**(1):1-9.

Smith, V. K., W. H. Desvousges, F. R. Johnson, and A. Fisher (1990), 'Can public information programs affect risk perceptions?,' *Journal of Policy Analysis and Management*, **9**:41-59.

Sun, H. (1990), *An Economic Analysis of Groundwater Pollution By Agricultural Chemicals*, Unpublished Master of Science Thesis, Department of Agricultural Economics, University of Georgia.

Viscusi, W. K., and C. J. O'Connor (1984), 'Adaptive responses to chemical labeling: are workers bayesian decision makers?,' *American Economic Review*, 74:942-956.

Wu, J. and B. Babcock (1995), 'Optimal design of a voluntary green payment program under asymmetric information,' *Journal of Agricultural and Resource Economics*, **20**: 316-27.

4. Measuring the Value of Protecting Ground Water Quality from Nitrate Contamination in Southeastern Pennsylvania

Donald J. Epp and Willard Delavan

INTRODUCTION

Southeastern Pennsylvania contains some of the richest non-irrigated farmlands in the world. Intensive manure and chemical fertilizer applications have also resulted in some of the highest ground water nitrate levels recorded in the Northeast (USGS 1985). Over 50 percent of private wells and nearly a quarter of all public water supplies have at some time in the last five years violated the US federal nitrate standard of no more than 10 mg NO_3-N per liter. The dangers of high nitrate levels to human health have forced citizens in the region to confront the issue and begin seeking solutions. Effective solutions depend upon a limited but growing knowledge of the physical characteristics of ground water, the relationship between nitrates and human health, and the economic consequences of nitrate pollution.

This chapter addresses the economic consequences of nitrate pollution by reporting the results of a Pennsylvania case study examining willingness to pay (WTP) to protect ground water quality and factors affecting WTP. This estimated WTP is a measure of the benefits of a specific protection program. This chapter builds upon the previous two chapters and the general water quality valuation model presented in Chapter 1 of this book by estimating WTP and its covariates for a hypothetical ground water management program intended to protect the residents in the study area from nitrate contamination, and comparing different ways of eliciting WTP to test for anchoring (the tendency of respondents unfamiliar with a good to focus on some cue or clue in the questionnaire).

STUDY DESIGN

The Pennsylvania study employed three interesting research design ideas. The first was the inclusion of two forms of the valuation question. After a section of the questionnaire that provided information about ground water and the health hazards of nitrates in drinking water, one form of the valuation question presented a dichotomous-choice question (a yes or no question) with bid levels selected from pretests. The study employed an open-ended question as the second valuation question as was done in the Randall *et al.* study discussed in Chapter 5 (this book). The dichotomous-choice form of the valuation question was presented as:

The Ballot
> *The program would be funded by an additional tax collected from each household __each year for 10 years__. This money would be placed in a special fund and used only for the program to protect ground water quality. Scientists expect the program would cost your household __an annual extra payment of $_____.__*

Q20 *If the program were placed on the next election ballot, would you vote for the program or against it? (Circle **one** number)*
   *1 **Yes** — I would vote for the implementation of the program.*
   *2 **No** — I would vote against the implementation of the program*

Q21 *Scientists cannot be certain about program costs; the final cost could be more or less than $_____. If you voted **Yes to Q20** perhaps you would vote for the program at a higher cost. If you voted **No to Q20** perhaps you would vote Yes at some lower cost or, perhaps the program would have to cost zero ($ 0) before you would vote for it. **What is the highest program cost at which you would __vote Yes?__ Please write your answer below.__***

> *I would __vote for__ the program if it cost __a maximum of $_____ in an annual tax for 10 years.*

The second form of the valuation question presented information about the average cost per household of local government expenditures for safety related activities, such as fire protection, police services and the construction and maintenance of streets and highways and followed this with an open-ended question about the maximum amount the respondent's household would be willing to pay for a plan to protect ground water quality. The annual expenditures for these services cover approximately the same range of dollar values as was used in the dichotomous choice initial bids. The wording of this form of the valuation question was as follows.

The Ballot

*The program would be funded by an additional tax collected **each year for ten years**. This money would be placed in a special fund and used only for the program of providing voluntary technical and financial assistance to farmers, homeowners, and other landowners to protect ground water from potential nitrate contamination.*

When making your decision, please keep in mind:
- *your household income*
- *your household expenditures on all other goods and services*
- *average **local government expenditures** for a family of four per year for:*
  - *police services are $208*
  - *fire protection are $64*
  - *parks and recreation are $31*
  - *streets and highways are $167*
  - *total local government expenditures are $820*

Q20   *What is the highest **annual payment** the program could cost your household at which you would vote **Yes**? Please write this amount in the space below.*
          $_____.

The study includes an innovative tactic to check for information bias similar to the methodology in the Poe and Bishop study discussed in Chapter 3 (this book). Information bias refers to potential errors in valuation stemming from either a lack of information about the good we are asking respondents to value or from providing information respondents did not have beforehand. We attempted to minimize the first type of information bias as much as possible for two reasons. First, we wanted to insure that responses were from individuals who are at least minimally knowledgeable about ground water and nitrates. Second, minimizing information bias may reduce random noise in WTP. A short quiz follows the information section of the questionnaire to verify respondents' knowledge of the subject (Figure 4.1). While this test does not distinguish between knowledge that respondents already possessed and information they acquired through reading the material provided, knowing that respondents understand the good to be valued may enhance the validity of the value estimation.

In order to **check the effectiveness of the information provided** we would like to ask you a few questions about ground water contamination. Please answer each question using the preceding information whenever you wish.

Q13   What percentage of public water supplies in your area comes from ground water? (please circle one)
      1 100%   2 80%   3 60%

Q14   Nitrates come from which of the following sources (circle **all** that apply)
      1 Fertilizer   2 home septic systems 3 sewage treatment plants

Q15   Blue baby syndrome:(Circle **all** that apply)
      1   Reduces the ability of blood to carry oxygen
      2   Is sometimes fatal in infants
      3   Only affects infants <u>over</u> six months old.

Q16   The US EPA is not convinced at this time that nitrates present a potential risk of cancer. (Circle **one**)
      1 True   2 False

Q17   Ground water is pumped out of water saturated soils which are like 'wet sponges' and 'veins'. (Circle **one**)
      1 True   2 False

Q18   Ground water comes from the land surface directly above. It does not spread to other areas. (Circle **one**)
      1 True   2 False

Figure 4.1. Information quiz, Pennsylvania case study

Another innovation was to ask respondents to evaluate the likelihood that the water in the study area will remain safe to drink over the next 10 years, first if the program described were approved and second, if the program were not approved. Although we recognize that safety in drinking water is a combination of the probability of consuming contaminated water, the probability that the contamination will adversely affect the consumer, and the importance the consumer places on those adverse effects, we chose not to specify these technical aspects of safety to the respondent at this point in the questionnaire. Rather, the answers are based on whatever came to mind as the respondents answered the question. Earlier in the questionnaire, prior to the valuation question, the choice scenario indicated that the program would reduce the probability of a specific well being contaminated from 50% to 25%. Respondents may have remembered this specification of the probability of contamination as they evaluated the likelihood that their water would be safe with and without the program. The response to each question was marked on a line representing probabilities ranging from 0% to 100%. The difference in the two ratings was used as an independent variable when analyzing willingness-to-pay responses.   This variable measures the subjective perceptions of the effectiveness of the program. Some previous ground water quality valuation studies have considered the effects of subjective risk perceptions (Edwards, 1988; Sun *et al.*, 1992).   Most prior water quality valuation studies assume individuals take the effects of proposed protection programs as certain.

DATA COLLECTION

The survey was conducted by the authors in the summer of 1996 in a manner adapted from Dillman's Total Design Method (1978).   Three mailings were sent at the recommended intervals to 1000 households chosen randomly from telephone listings in rural portions of Lebanon and Lancaster counties in Pennsylvania. The sample was split equally between those receiving the two formats.   The overall response rate was 68%.   Useable questionnaires were received from 617 respondents; 284 (63%) for the Dichotomous Choice (DOE) format and 333 (75%) for the Informed Open-Ended (IOE) format.   The response rate for the IOE format was statistically significantly higher than the response rate for the DOE format.

Prior to administering the survey, the research team used verbal protocols and pretests of questionnaire items to test whether respondents understood what was asked and to obtain a bid range for policies to protect ground water quality. Results of the preliminary investigations were combined with results from similar efforts in Georgia and Maine described in Chapter 2 (this book) to design the final questionnaire.

PROTEST BIDS AND ALTERNATIVE TREATMENTS

Before presenting the data used in this study, it is important to make clear the way we calculated the mean and median willingness to pay. The method to use for calculating the mean or median willingness to pay from survey data is still being discussed by practitioners.   Two key questions which can have considerable significance in the results are (1) Should the bid of respondents who protested against some aspect of the valuation question or scenario be included in the calculation? and (2) What portion of the estimated response function should be used to calculate the mean willingness to pay?

Turning first to the initial question, one can find numerous arguments favoring deleting from the calculations the responses from those who indicated a protest. Indeed, the inclusion of screening questions to determine which respondents altered their valuation response due to a protest about some aspect of the task, was designed to eliminate the protest responses. The rationale for eliminating these responses was that they did not indicate the respondent's value of the nonmarket good in question, but rather, reflected values affected by the protest. If a large proportion of the responses in a particular study were classified as protests, it was thought that this raised questions about the appropriateness of the question format or the scenario. Alternatively, those who argue that the protest responses should be included in the data set for calculating mean or median willingness to pay usually do so for two reasons. First, even though it is common practice to include a question to screen for protest responses, there is no established mechanism for determining which responses to exclude. Second, many believe that the results more closely estimate the outcome of a referendum on the topic being studied. That is, a median willingness to pay calculated from data that include protest responses will indicate the maximum 'cost' that would still receive a favorable vote in a referendum.

It seems apparent that the two approaches are, at least in part, trying to estimate two different things. For those removing protest votes, the objective is to measure the value of a nonmarket good or service. In that case the protest responses introduce static in the estimation process by introducing considerations other than the value of the good in question. Those who advocate retaining the protest responses when calculating the mean or median values are interested in determining values that theoretically coincide with results of the most frequently employed way of determining policy — a legislative or public referendum. While each of these approaches has value, the differences point out the importance of clearly indicating the objective of the study and the treatment of protest responses. In this study we removed the protest responses from the data set when calculating mean willingness to pay. More discussion of this issue is provided by Randall *et al.* in Chapter 5 of this book and Bergstrom *et al.* in Chapter 2 of this book.

The second question — what portion of the estimated response function should be used when calculating mean and median values — is not so easily answered. The need for a decision stems from the fact that the proportion of 'yes' responses to a dichotomous-choice valuation question can be assumed to be distributed as a logistic function. This function indicates a very high probability of a 'yes' response to very low prices, but the probability of a 'yes' response declines as the price increases. The problem requiring a decision is that the logistic function has infinitely long tails asymptotic to one at low bid values and asymptotic to zero at high bid values. Thus, the area under the estimated logistic curve is infinite. Further, certain sets of response data result in logistic curve estimates where a substantial portion of the negative tail is significantly far from one. In fact, some data sets result in mean willingness-to-pay estimates that are negative. Conceptually, negative prices can be explained in theoretical economic discussions, but are problematic for policy-makers and others who may use the results of willingness-to-pay studies.

Two approaches have been employed to estimate the mean and median of the function. The first, employed by designers of statistical packages for estimating such values, is to truncate the tails of the estimated logistic curve at very large absolute values. These truncations permit a value to be estimated and the truncations are at points on the estimated logistic curve where altering the truncation point slightly would not substantially alter the calculated values. This procedure permits calculation of estimated mean and median willingness-to-pay values, though occasionally these estimated values are negative. This method is described by Cameron (1988). On the other hand, Hanemann (1984) presents a method which, in effect, truncates the estimated logistic curve at a zero price and at whatever price one chooses for an upper bound. This technique ensures that the estimated mean and median values are positive numbers. It also gives results that are trivially different from the Cameron method if, but only if, the estimated probability of a 'yes' answer at a zero price is virtually one and the upper truncation is at very high values of the bid price. Only in cases where the negative tail of the estimated curve is substantially far from one will estimates differ significantly.

Table 4.1 illustrates the issue discussed here. The economic analyst must choose a method for dealing with protest responses and an approach for calculating mean or median willingness to pay. The WTP values indicated in the table are from the Pennsylvania study reported in this chapter. They illustrate the differences in mean WTP produced by the various choices. In the analysis reported in this chapter we have chosen the approach that will lead to conservative estimates of value; remove the protest responses and calculate the value of mean willingness to pay using the Cameron approach.

Table 4.1. Estimates of mean willingness to pay, Pennsylvania case study

	Cameron Approach	Haneman Approach
	(Confidence intervals)	
Include protest responses	$34 (± $83)	$255(± $31)
Remove protest responses	$70 (± $10)	$104 (± $10)

DATA ANALYSIS

Our analysis consists of two parts. The first part looks at simple descriptive statistics and outlines the important variables in the analysis. One highlight of the first part is the results of the information quiz. The second part examines the determinants of WTP and compares the two elicitation formats, each using censored regression with the open-ended responses of the IOE and DOE questions as the dependent variable.

DESCRIPTIVE STATISTICS

Socioeconomic Characteristics and Water Use

Approximately 70% of study respondents were male. The mean age of respondents was 52. The average number of people living in the responding households was two. Few (12 or 2%) of the respondents were expecting someone in the household to give birth in the coming months. Thirty-nine respondents (6%) indicated that they were involved in farming. Over half (62%) of those responding had a high school education or less. Approximately one-quarter of those answering had a college or professional degree. One-quarter of all respondents were retired, over half were fully employed (57%) and approximately 10% were unemployed. A majority (68%) of households had incomes below $30,000 per year, although a significant portion (26%) are in the $40,000 to $50,000 range.

Over half of the respondents had lived in the study area for over nineteen years, two-thirds for over ten years. Approximately three-quarters of the respondents lived in a township while approximately one-quarter of the respondents resided in a borough or city. Over half the respondents indicated that they would probably not move from the study area while approximately two- thirds of the respondents indicated that there was less than a 50% probability that they would move in the next ten years.

Roughly two-fifths of the respondents used private wells as their major source of drinking water, and the remaining three-fifths used public water sources (systems subject to government testing and safety standards) in the form of a private community well system, a public water system, or bottled water. Nearly a quarter of the respondents had installed a water softener within the past five years. Similarly, almost a quarter had installed a pollution protection device, such as a water filter on their tap or point of entry. Few (4%) had installed a new well in the last five years, and 6 percent had boiled water from their tap (presumably for infant formula, since no major contamination incidents had required them to do so). Almost half (44%) had purchased bottled water at sometime in the previous five years.

Perceptions of Water Safety
On a scale of 0 to 100 (0 = definitely not safe, 50 = maybe safe and 100 = definitely safe) the mean response for drinking water safety at the present time was 71, about half way between maybe safe and definitely safe. About one-quarter of the respondents fell in the maybe safe range between 40 and 60. When asked to rate their perception of water safety if the program was implemented and if it was not implemented on a scale of 0 to 100, the mean difference between the two was 8.5, indicating that in general respondents felt that the program would be successful in increasing drinking water safety. There were 102 respondents (16%) who believed that their water would be less safe with the program than without it.

Respondents were generally concerned for the safety of drinking water as it relates to different groups of people. For each group of people who might be affected by water quality (themselves, their family living with them, family living in the study area but not with them, other people in the study area, and future generations who might live in the study area) over three-quarters of the respondents answered that they were at least somewhat concerned for each.

This concern is reinforced by how respondents answered a question about their priority for local government spending to address each of a list of possible problems, including protecting drinking water quality. Three-quarters (75%) of all respondents listed protecting drinking water quality as a high or very high priority for local government spending.

Respondents indicated a generally high level of concern for five sources of contamination (leakage from community sewage plants; leakage from private home septic systems; leakage from fertilizer applied to farms, private lawns and gardens or golf courses; leakage from farm livestock wastes; and leakage from landfills and garbage dumps). Over 50 percent of all respondents were concerned or very concerned about all five sources. Leakage from farm livestock wastes had the highest number of concerned or very concerned answers with almost three-quarters (71%), followed by contamination from fertilizer (70%) and leakage from landfills and garbage dumps (64%).

Bid Means by Question Format
Two hundred and eighty-four responses were received for the dichotomous choice followed by open-ended (DOE) format. The open-ended responses range from $0 to $1,000, with 114 zero bids. The mean bid (WTP) for the open-ended portion of the question was $45. The calculated mean WTP for the dichotomous choice portion of the DOE format was $70.

For the informed open-ended (IOE) format, 333 questionnaires were analyzed. Bids ranged from $0 to $967, with 151 zero bids (45%). The mean was $29. These calculations do not exclude protest bids.

Respondents who bid zero were asked why they bid zero. Approximately one-fifth (22%) of the 265 who bid zero did so because they did not feel the program would be effective. Few (12%) did not believe the program was necessary and even fewer (8%) stated that the program was not worth the cost to them. Nearly 20% did not feel comfortable with the idea of paying into a special fund to protect the environment. Although asked to circle only one answer many respondents (110 or 35% of zero bidders) gave more than one response. These answers were coded either to fit into one of the provided answers or were included in one of three additional categories (i) dissatisfaction with government or taxes, (ii) protest related to farming, and (iii) other (list available upon request from the authors).

Prior Information and Knowledge of Ground Water

Information is important in reducing uncertainty. Ideally, any information provided should remind the respondent of what they already know about ground water and nitrates (otherwise information could be unduly influencing WTP), be easy to understand and not overly lengthy. Our central concern is not whether respondents actually read the information we present them, but instead that they know something about what we are asking them to value. Respondents who have a better handle on this information are more likely to diligently search their preferences and make an attempt at ordering them.

During verbal protocol sessions it was clear that in many cases respondents did not have a basic understanding of the change in ground water safety which the program represented. Respondents who did not read the information provided may have had a different perception of what it was we were asking them to value. Bids from those who did not read or understand the information should not be treated as valid responses, and arguably should not be included. A test of whether willingness to pay differs for those who read and understood the information was conducted versus willingness to pay of those who did not understand the information by simply including different measures of understanding about ground water issues in regressions. We expected a wider variance in WTP from the uninformed as well as a higher percentage of zero bids. Information was not a significant determinant of WTP but did have an effect on the number of zero bids.

Approximately 40% of respondents had had their water tested in the past five years while 40% had not and 20% did not know whether or not their water had been tested. Only one-third of respondents knew of chemical treatment of water (i.e. chlorination). This indicates a low awareness of a well-publicized regulation, because all public drinking water supplies (except for bottled water) in Pennsylvania must be chlorinated.

Approximately 31% indicated that they had received information about potential nitrate contamination in their county prior to this study. Two hundred and thirty-seven (38.4%) indicated that they had received information about the possible connection between nitrates in drinking water and human health prior to this study. This may indicate that the information provided in the questionnaire is new to over half of the respondents who scored high on the information check.

The respondents' understanding of ground water and the proposed ground water protection program was revealed in the information quiz section (see Figure 4.1 for the text of the questions). The results for the quiz/check were encouraging overall (see Table 4.2). The low percentage of correct answers on question 13 could be explained by poor question wording; where the question reads 'what percentage of water in your area comes from ground water', it should read 'what percentage in the study area'. Respondents make their own frame as to what area they are estimating even though the correct answer, 80%, is listed in the information section. Questions 14 and 15 also seemed to present some difficulties for some respondents. Although we cannot test this, there is a possibility that some respondents were reluctant to circle more than one answer even though the question asked them to circle all that apply.

One possible explanation for the overall encouraging correct answer rate for the information quiz is the wording of the introduction. The introduction was crafted so that respondents were encouraged to go back to the information section. This may have persuaded them to read it if they had not, or to read or at least browse it a second time if they had in fact read it the first time. Care was taken to not insult the reader although that danger existed, especially since the questions themselves were almost word for word from the section. Some respondents indicated a general distrust for government, as well as offering critiques of paranoid academics. In general though, the number of missing values for the information quiz was low, ranging from 5 to 10% of the surveys received.

Table 4.2. Percentage of correct responses to information quiz, Pennsylvania case study

Question Number (See Figure 4.1)	Frequency Correct	Percent Correct	Missing	Percent Correct Adjusted for Missing Values
13	296	53.6	65	48.0
14	409	70.3	35	66.3
15	451	80.8	59	73.1
16	511	88.4	11.6	82.8
17	543	93.5	36	88.0
18	560	96.7	38	90.8

ELICITATION FORMAT AND WILLINGNESS TO PAY

In this section the mean willingness to pay was calculated from the answers to the open-ended question in each format to determine whether or not elicitation format has an effect on willingness to pay. In theory the results would exhibit convergent validity if outcomes were invariant to elicitation. The literature suggests that elicitation does affect willingness to pay. Opponents of contingent valuation claim that this shortcoming invalidates the method. Proponents maintain that values will differ when a valuation question is worded differently and that the object to be valued is different. When the ultimate purpose is to provide estimates of value, and no markets exist for the good in question, different values may arise from different elicitation formats and should be examined.

In this analysis we remove protest bids and observations with missing values and estimate the best model using tobit regression. Removing protests affects the mean WTP reported earlier in the chapter. The mean WTP of respondents receiving the DOE format was $74 with a standard deviation of $125. The responses to the IOE format had a mean WTP of $51 with a standard deviation of $92. These mean values are statistically significantly different from each other ($\alpha=0.1$) and the remainder of this section presents results of analyses to examine the factors affecting WTP and the possible reasons for this difference.

The independent variables are defined as follows: Perceived effectiveness of the program is the difference between the perceived level of safety with the program and the perceived level of safety without the program ($\Delta H_2OSAFETY$). Income (I) is a categorical variable although it is treated as a continuous variable by using the midpoint values of each income category. PROACTIVE, another dummy variable, indicates that respondents have taken some type of averting action to avoid health risks due to ground water contamination in the past 5 years. PRIVATE WATER is a dichotomous variable representing the type of water supply as private well or public supply.

Other independent variables were considered initially, but were eliminated when their coefficient estimates were not significantly different from zero in any of the regressions. The eliminated variables were: the presence of children in the household, concern for drinking water safety (a dummy variable equal to one if the respondent both places a high priority on local government expenditures for ground water protection and is concerned about ground water safety), age of the respondent, and gender of the respondent.

We examined the socioeconomic characteristics of the respondents of the two sub-samples to determine if they are comparable. If the population means of various characteristics differ for the two sub-samples, it may indicate problems with sample selection and will complicate comparisons of the estimated beta coefficients. T-tests of the relevant variables show that there is no significant difference between the two samples on any item except the measure of WTP.

The regression is a censored (tobit) regression using the open-ended valuation question. The regression results are listed in Table 4.3. The IOE regression (second column) shows that ΔH_2O SAFETY is significant at the 0.01 level while income (I) is significant at the 0.05 level or better. Neither PROACTIVE (=1 if the respondent conducted some type of averting activity in the last five years) nor PRIVATE WELL were statistically significant.

Table 4.3. Tobit Regressions marginal effects, Pennsylvania case study

Variable name	IOE n = 178	DOE n = 162	DOE with DC-BID n = 162
CONSTANT	-25.7236[c] (13.5520)	-30.6890[c] (18.2206)	-63.4601[a] (17.8559)
ΔH_2OSAFETY	0.9671[a] (0.2049)	1.3504[a] (0.2812)	1.3659[a] (0.2599)
I (thousands)	0.3862[b] (0.2005)	0.6782[b] (0.2931)	0.7064[a] (0.2721)
PROACTIVE	15.5406 (11.2027)	40.6702[b] (15.7884)	37.0425[a] (14.6893)
PRIVATE WATER	0.4469 (10.4673)	-25.5094[c] (15.6498)	-29.1403[b] (14.6046)
DC-BID			.2289[a] (0.0456)
log-likelihood	-1047.3182	-995.5910	-978.9932
pseudo R-squared	0.1880	0.2639	0.3719

Notes
[a]significant at the 1 percent level; [b]significant at the 5 percent level; [c]significant at the 10 percent level. Standard errors in parentheses.

In contrast, the third and fourth columns show the results of the same model using data from the open-ended portion of the DOE format. The DOE elicitation format appears to capture the relationship between WTP and the independent variables better both without (third column) and with the inclusion of DC-BID (fourth column) than does the IOE format. This may be because the DOE format is more market-like than the IOE.

All independent variables are significant at the 0.05 level or better with the exception of PRIVATE WATER which is significant at the 0.10 level in the third column.

We had hypothesized that private well owners would bid higher than those on municipal supplies but the null hypothesis, that there is no significant difference between the two groups, is rejected. The negative sign on the coefficient may be due to an erroneous perception of the good being valued (they may perceive that ground water protection is their private responsibility). Or, it could be due to the influence of those who have had well tests that were negative for nitrates.

If we include the initial bid or payment amount (fourth column) as an independent variable (DC-BID) the McKelvey and Zavoina (1975) pseudo r-squared[1] increases from 0.26 to 0.37. The estimated coefficient for DC-BID is highly significant with the expected sign. This shows that a large degree of variation may be explained by the starting bid. This points to a positive starting point or anchoring bias (Boyle *et al.* 1985, Bishop and Heberlein 1986).

The test for starting point bias is straightforward.

$$WTP \ (X; \ \beta) \ = \ WTP \ (X; \ \beta, \ \beta_s)$$
$$H_0 : \beta_s = 0 \tag{4.1}$$

The t-statistic (5.02) is significant at the 0.01 level, rejecting the null hypothesis and indicating that the requested payment in the dichotomous choice format serves as a significant determinant of respondents' WTP. Randall *et al.* (Chapter 5 this book) also report evidence of anchoring effects in open-ended valuation responses that follow a dichotomous choice valuation question.

Survey design could have influenced this result. More respondents answered no to the dichotomous choice question and offered a lower amount in the second part than answered yes and offered a higher amount.

A likelihood ratio test rejected the null hypothesis that the two elicitation formats measure the same underlying preferences. In other words, the elicitation format significantly affects responses.

IMPLICATIONS AND CONCLUSIONS

This chapter has practical applications in terms of what the results can contribute both to informed policy making and to research methods. Specifically, the chapter results can be targeted to assist policy makers and researchers answer two specific questions. What is ground water protection worth? What research implications in terms of methodology can be gained from this work?

Policy makers may be interested in an aggregate measure of the benefits of protecting ground water from nitrates in the study area. A complete answer would include the range of estimates and factors affecting WTP. Estimates of mean and median WTP for the study region are between zero and $67 depending upon how the question is asked and whether or not protest bids are included. Aggregate measures ranged from zero to 5.1 million annually or 51 million for the ten year contribution period. The mean WTP is significantly different from zero. Several factors significantly influence WTP: income (+), perceptions of increased safety with the program (+), prior action to protect household water via averting activity (+) and private well ownership (-). Surprisingly, the presence of children in the household and concern for drinking water safety do not affect WTP. Also, neither age nor gender affect WTP.

The range of estimated WTP ($0-$73) may be unacceptable to policy makers because of its imprecision. When selecting from this range, one must recognize that the IOE format may lack market realism and the DOE format suffers from significant anchoring bias. In this study we believe that policy recommendations should be based on the IOE format.

The final figure policy makers choose depends upon the treatment of protest bidders. Since protest bidders, by definition, have not offered a valuation for protecting ground water, the authors believe that protest bids should be excluded and the mean WTP estimate of $51 should be used. This opinion is based upon the assumption that protest bidders are not addressing the value of ground water protection.

Another significant finding of the Pennsylvania study is the importance of the respondent's subjective perception of the effectiveness of the program. The more effective the program is perceived to be, the more people are willing to pay for the program. This is not astonishing in and of itself, but surprising in that the role of uncertainty and its measurement are not often applied in this type of research. In most instances, respondents are assumed to accept the outcome of the hypothetical program as certain. This study shows that consumers are skeptical, but are willing to pay something even when they are not certain of a favorable outcome.

Finally, questionnaire design can significantly influence willingness-to-pay responses in a CVM study. In this study we attempted to isolate anchoring bias by reducing other potential sources of bias, such as information about the nature of the good to be valued. Our approach was to include basic information about the good, to test knowledge of the subject to encourage respondent consideration of the information, and to carefully design questions to elicit a valuation response. We controlled for bias that might result from differing non-use and aesthetic values by examining a good with little or no perceived non-use value.

The elicitation format that included a dichotomous choice question followed by an open-ended question exhibited significantly higher WTP bids than did the informed open-ended format. Anchoring appears to be the principal factor in the difference between the results of the two elicitation formats. These results suggest that the differing average WTP bids are due in large part to survey design. Thus, it appears that providing an open-ended question as the second part of a double bounded dichotomous choice bid elicitation format does not avoid the anchoring bias associated with the dichotomous choice. Future research should test whether other combinations of elicitation formats yield more consistent estimates. For example, hybrids of polychotomous choice as suggested by Poe and Welsh (1996) with the informed open-ended follow up may be promising.

NOTES

1. The McKelvey and Zavoina R^2 is:

$$R_{MZ}^2 = \frac{\sum_{i=1}^{n} (\hat{Y}_i^* - \bar{Y}_i^*)^2}{\sum_{i=1}^{n} (\hat{Y}_i^* - \bar{Y}_i^*)^2 + N \delta^2}$$

REFERENCES

Bishop, Richard C. and Thomas A. Heberlein (1986), 'Does contingent valuation work?' in Cummings, Ronald G., David S. Brookshire, and William D. Schulze (eds) *Valuing Public Goods: The Contingent Valuation Method,* Totowa, New Jersey: Rowman and Allan Held Publishers.

Boyle, Kevin J., Richard C. Bishop and Michael P. Welsh (1985), 'Starting point bias in contingent valuation bidding games' *Land Economics,* **61**(1):321-30.

Cameron, T.A. (1988), 'A new paradigm for valuing non-marketed goods using referendum data: maximum likelihood estimation by censored logistic regression,' *Journal of Environmental Economics and Management,* **15**(3):355-79.

Dillman, Don A. (1978), *Mail and Telephone Surveys: The Total Design Method,* New York: Wiley.

Edwards, S. F. (1988), 'Option prices for groundwater protection,' *Journal of Environmental Economics and Management*, **15**:475-81.

Hanemann, W.M. (1984), 'Welfare evaluations in contingent valuation experiments with discrete responses,' *American Journal of Agricultural Economics*, **66** (3): 332-41.

McKelvey, R. and W. Zavoina (1975), 'A statistical model for the analysis of ordinal level dependent variables,' *Journal of Mathematical Sociology*, **4**:103-20.

Poe, Gregory L., and Michael P. Welsh (1996), *Uncertainty in contingent values and procedural variance across elicitation formats: a multiple bounded discrete choice approach*, Working Paper 96-03, Cornell University.

Sun, H., J.C. Bergstrom, and J.H. Dorfman (1992), 'Estimating the benefits of groundwater contamination control,' *Southern Journal of Agricultural Economics*, **24**(2):63-70.

United States Geological Survey (1985), *Occurrence of nitrate and herbicides in ground water in the Upper Conestoga River Basin, Pennsylvania*. Water Resources Investigations Report 85-4202. Prepared in cooperation with the USDA and Pennsylvania Department of Environmental Resources.

5. Ground Water, Surface Water, and Wetlands Valuation in Ohio

Alan Randall, Damitha DeZoysa, and Side Yu

INTRODUCTION

The overall objective of the research reported in this chapter was to perform a comprehensive split-sample contingent valuation (CV) study that would estimate benefits of three environmental services: enhancements to ground water, surface water and wetland habitat. While ground water was a primary focus, this effort continues a long-standing research program addressing the relationships among components of complex policy packages (Hoehn and Randall, 1989; Randall and Hoehn, 1996). The analysis and discussion builds upon the general water quality valuation model presented in Chapter 1 (this book) by testing empirical hypotheses using multivariate analysis of the relationship between vote responses to an offered protection program and a set of explanatory variables, and testing hypotheses concerning the value relationships among components of multipart policies. In addition, continuous WTP responses were examined to address the effect of referendum offer price, functional form and the relative magnitudes of mean and median WTP from referendum vs. continuous WTP response data.

PROGRAMS OFFERED

Three protection programs were offered in our case study: stabilization and reduction of nitrate levels in ground water in the Maumee River basin in northwestern Ohio (GW); reduction of sediments due to soil erosion, in streams and lakes in the Maumee River basin (SW); and protection and enhancement of wetlands along the shore of the western basin of Lake Erie (WI). The baseline and with-program situations were described in considerable detail in the survey instruments, followed in each case by a box containing a diagram showing baseline and with-program situations and a brief verbal summary (Figure 5.1).

In each case, the program would be financed by a one-time tax with the proceeds dedicated to funding the program. For GW and SW, the funds would provide incentives for farmers to adopt environmentally benign crop-growing practices. For WI, wetlands easements would be purchased.

STUDY DESIGN

Three populations were sampled: Maumee drainage rural residents, Maumee drainage urban residents, and residents of Columbus and Cleveland SMAs; the latter sample provided observations of the out-of-region population. Zip codes in the relevant regions, population-weighted, were selected randomly. Individuals were then randomly selected from Ohio Bureau of Motor Vehicles lists for the selected zip codes and cleansed of duplicate last names with the same address. In all, 1050 names were selected; 350 for each population.

The study design was entirely split-sample, with each sample member receiving a single proposal (to provide one, two, or three of GW, SW, and/or WI, as the case may be) and a single tax-price. In all, 147 versions of the survey instrument were used: 3 populations x 7 proposals x 7 prices (Figure 5.2). Prices used were selected following an open-ended pretest, using the DWEABS method (Cooper 1993) which over-weights prices near the *ex ante* expected mean and median WTP. Prices used were $0.25, $10, $30, $54, $80, $120, and $200. Ultimately, observations at the $0.25 price were dropped from the analysis because as other researchers have observed, responses at unrealistically low prices tend to be somewhat unstable (Krosnick 1991).

Following a one-shot referendum at a tax-price randomly assigned, open-ended WTP was reported for each respondent. Values obtained are total values, with no formal basis for separating use and passive-use values. One may surmise, however, that the out-of-region sample may have been motivated by passive use to a greater degree than the other samples.

SURVEY ADMINISTRATION

Following several focus groups and a field pretest, surveys were mailed to the selected samples. The Dillman total design method was followed, to the extent permitted by a strictly-limited budget. The major items omitted from the

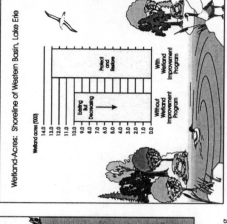

Wetland-Acres: Shoreline of Western Basin, Lake Erie

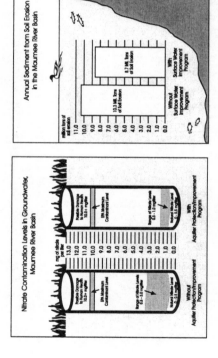

Nitrate Contamination Levels in Groundwater, Maumee River Basin

Annual Sediment from Soil Erosion in the Maumee River Basin

Without the aquifer protection/ improvement program, typical nitrate levels in groundwater are below the EPA 10 mg per liter Maximum Contaminant Level, but are higher than "natural" levels. With the proposed program nitrate levels would be reduced, and eventually stabilized between one-half (0.5) and one mg per liter.

Without the surface water improvement program, the sediment and nutrients going into the Maumee River Basin and Lake Erie would cause deterioration, siltation, water pollution and reduction of fish and wildlife habitat. With the proposed program the volume of sediment entering the Maumee River would be reduced by about 15 percent, thereby reducing the load of sediment in the shipping channel. Recreation in and near the river would be enhanced and the quality of water supplied to Toledo, Maumee and Perrysburg would be improved.

Without the wetland improvement program, wetland acreage and the wildlife habitat would decrease. The proposed program would protect and improve existing wetlands, restore 3,000 additional acres of wetlands, and provide about 20 percent more wildlife habitat for migrating birds and waterfowl.

Figure 5.1. Ground water, surface water and wetlands protection programs, Ohio case study.

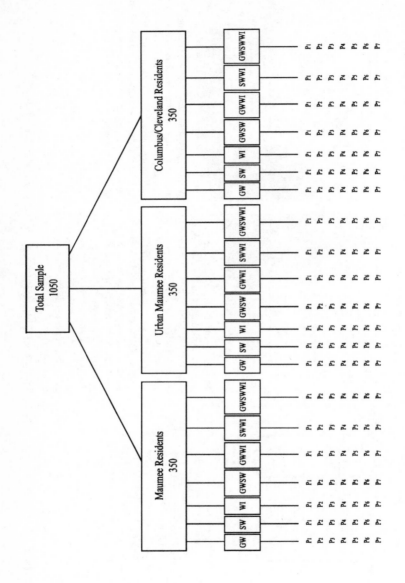

Figure 5.2. Sampling design for Ohio case study

Dillman procedure were the use of incentives to respond, the final certified package to persistent nonrespondents after several mailings, and reminder post-cards.

Results

The overall response rate was 51 percent of delivered questionnaires; for the different populations, response rates were 58 percent for Maumee rural, 50 percent for Maumee urban, and 44 percent for Columbus and Cleveland.

After discarding questionnaires with item non-response to the referendum, 427 questionnaires remained: responses to the one-shot referendum were 201 yes, 114 no, and 112 protest-no. This rather large 'protest-no' vote was unexpected. One could guess at the reasons, and three possibilities have some appeal: (1) some respondents were uncomfortable with the idea of subsidizing farmers to use environmentally benign production methods; (2) the multi-county program region was not consistent with the ordinary taxing jurisdictions, i.e., county or state; and (3) in a mail survey, a follow-up question inviting protest-voters to self-identify may actually influence the voting behavior of respondents who 'read ahead' before answering.

Standard practice is to discard 'protest-no' voters, treating them as nonrespondents, (i.e., people whose vote does not reflect their WTP). However, our initial econometric analyses of voting behavior suggested that 'protest-no' voters were more similar, attitudinally and demographically, to 'no' voters than to 'yes' voters.[1] This provides a motivation for retaining all 'no' voters including protesters in the sample for subsequent analysis. Accordingly, we provide results for two samples, which we label YN(n = 315, yes: 201, and no: 114) and YNP (n = 427, yes: 201, and no + protest-no: 226). For multivariate analysis, missing data for right-hand side variables (RHS) reduced these sample sizes to YN: 286, and YNP: 377.

Multivariate analysis was conducted using the probit choice function and maximum likelihood estimation procedures with the left-hand-side variable (LHS) indicating a respondent's 'yes' or 'no' vote. Definitions of choice variables used in the choice function are as follows.

LHS :	VOTE	:	yes= 1; 0 otherwise
RHS :	SAMP1	:	Maumee rural sample = 1; 0 otherwise
	SAMP2	:	Maumee urban sample = 1; 0 otherwise
	SAMP3	:	Columbus and Cleveland sample = 1; 0 otherwise
	LPS12	:	log of tax-price interacted with SAMP1 or SAMP2
	LPS3	:	log of tax price interacted with SAMP3
	I	:	household income
	GENDER	:	male = 1; 0 otherwise
	EDUCA1	:	not graduate high school = 1; 0 otherwise

EDUCA3   :   has college degree = 1; 0 otherwise
GW1   :   high priority for water quality programs = 1; 0
               otherwise
GW3   :   low priority for water quality programs = 1; 0
               otherwise
WHP1   :   high priority of wetlands protection = 1; 0
               otherwise
WHP3   :   low priority for wetlands protection = 1; 0
               otherwise
EVH1   :   government should spend more on education =
               1; 0 otherwise
EVH3   :   government should spend less on education; 0
               otherwise
FU   :   expects future visits to program region = 1; 0
               otherwise
V1   :   GW program = 1; 0 otherwise
V2   :   SW program = 1; 0 otherwise
V3   :   WI program = 1; 0 otherwise
V4   :   GW WI programs = 1; 0 otherwise
V5   :   GW SW programs = 1; 0 otherwise
V6   :   SW WI programs = 1; 0 otherwise

Results obtained in Table 5.1 were consistent with prior expectations with a few exceptions related to significance of the estimates. The price variable (logged, and combined with sample dummies to permit the price response to differ across samples) is a highly significant predictor of the respondents' voting behavior. The out-of-region sample exhibited the most price-sensitive voting response. The income coefficient was positive and significant. Attitudinal variables indicating high priority for water quality and wetland protection, desire to increase public spending on education, health and vocational training programs, and the expectation of future visits to the region (in the case of YNP data) were positively correlated with VOTE and statistically significant. All the program dummy variables had the expected sign compared to the omitted program (GWSWWI), failing to reject monotonicity – i.e., *ceteris paribus,* more public goods are preferred to fewer – however, only V1 was significant. With YN data, 74 percent of vote responses were predicted correctly, while with YNP data the corresponding result was 71 percent (Table 5.2). However, the YNP model predicted the actual counts of 'yes' vs. 'no' votes more accurately.

Median and Mean WTP
The standard measures of central tendency for WTP are the median and mean, which can be interpreted respectively in terms of a voting criterion (WTP of the median voting household) and the potential Pareto-improvement criterion (benefit equals mean WTP aggregated across

households). Median WTP/household, estimated with the YNP data set, is reported in Table 5.3 for each of the seven programs/combinations, pooled across the three samples, and for each of the three samples pooled across programs. As other researchers have observed (e.g., Haab and McConnell 1997), the log-normal probit model often provides a good fit of the vote data within the range of tax-prices assigned, but generates absurdly high estimates of mean WTP. Lower bound means (LBM), which assume effectively that all incremental 'yes' votes as the tax-price is reduced apply only to the lower end-point in each given range of tax-prices, are reported (Table 5.3).

Observe that while sample 3 (Columbus and Cleveland) had the highest estimated median WTP, it had the lowest LBM. This is consistent with the estimated probit model (Table 5.2), in which sample 3 has the highest intercept and the steepest tax-price slope.

Multi-component programs

The literature on valuation of multi-component programs is replete with empirical reports that WTP for a multi-component program is less than the sum of WTP for its components evaluated independently. What is controversial is the interpretation of this phenomenon. Diamond (1996) and Kahneman and Knetsch (1992), seeing no theoretical reason for this phenomenon, regard it as evidence of a pathology in contingent valuation. However, Randall and Hoehn (1996), Hoehn and Loomis (1993), Hoehn (1991), and Hoehn and Randall (1989) provide arguments that standard economic concepts — constrained budgets, and substitution among policy components — can be expected to induce the observed relationship. Randall and Hoehn (1996) demonstrate the predicted relationships with numerical simulations using an estimated system of market demands.

Comparing estimated median WTP across programs (Table 5.3) we observe that GWSWWI is higher-valued than any single-component or two-component program; GWWI is higher-valued than GW or WI; GWSW is higher-valued than GW or SW; and SWWI is higher-valued than WI. However, in every case the value of the multi-component program is less than the sum of the values of its components evaluated separately. The one exception to this pattern of results is SWWI which is lower-valued than SW. This result seems to be an artifact of our small sample size for such an elaborate split-sample design: non-response rate was abnormally high for SWWI at prices of $80 and higher (76% vs. 49% for the overall survey), an event which may well have been random.

Using the Wald test, we rejected the following null hypotheses: GW ≥ GWSW, and GW = SW = WI = GWWI = GWSW = SWWI = GWSWWI. For SW ≥ SWWI, the sign was 'wrong,' in that the results supported the null rather than the expected (alternative) hypothesis. For all other pairs of

Table 5.1: Multivariate Probit analysis, Ohio case study

	YN data			YNP data		
	Parameter Estimate	p-value	Variable Mean	Parameter Estimate	p-value	Variable Mean
CONSTANT	1.0073	0.12		0.5071	0.36	
LPS12	-0.341	0.00[a]	2.7985	-0.3265	0.00[a]	2.9144
LPS3	-0.7556	0.00[a]	1.0897	-0.7119	0.00[a]	1.0165
I	0.000009	0.01[a]	40808	0.000009	0.00[a]	39749
GENDER	-0.2763	0.12	0.4860	-0.2358	0.11	0.4987
EDUCA1	-0.0461	0.86	0.1329	0.0540	0.81	0.1300
EDUCA3	0.1512	0.46	0.3182	0.0824	0.63	0.3077
GW1	0.4085	0.02[a]	0.6154	0.4309	0.00[a]	0.5650
GW3	-0.3240	0.53	0.03450	-0.4953	0.24	0.0557
WHP1	0.5290	0.01[a]	0.3566	0.4825	0.00[a]	0.3130
WHP3	-0.8481	0.00[a]	0.1643	-0.8689	0.00[a]	0.2149
EHV1	0.3884	0.03[a]	0.6189	0.3111	0.04[a]	0.6048
EHV3	0.0376	0.92	0.0524	0.1080	0.75	0.0610
FU	0.3043	0.12	0.7098	0.3603	0.03[a]	0.6844
V1	-0.4993	0.13	0.1469	-0.5539	0.04[a]	0.1645

| | YN data | | | YNP data | | |
	Parameter Estimate	p-value	Variable Mean	Parameter Estimate	p-value	Variable Mean
V2	-0.0986	0.78	0.1189	-0.1755	0.54	0.1273
V3	-0.4887	0.15	0.1399	-0.4031	0.16	0.1300
V4	-0.1151	0.73	0.1399	-0.2543	0.36	0.1459
V5	-0.1169	0.71	0.1608	-0.0567	0.83	0.1565
V6	-0.5420	0.10[c]	0.1504	-0.3421	0.23	0.1406
SAMP1	0.07683	0.71	0.3636	0.0222	0.89	0.4005
SAMP3	1.6300	0.14	0.2867	1.6777	0.05[b]	0.2653

Notes
[a]significant at .01 level.
[b]significant at .05 level.
[c]significant at .10 level.

Table 5.2. Predicted vs. Actual votes, Ohio case study

		YN Data			YNP Data		
		Predicted		Total	Predicted		Total
		No	Yes		No	Yes	
Actual	No	52	52	104	138	57	195
	Yes	23	159	182	53	129	182
Total		75	211	286	191	186	377

Table 5.3. Estimated median and lower bound mean (LBM) WTP ($/household, one-time payment), YNP data, Ohio case study

Program	Sample	Median	LBM
GW	[a]	20.80	52.78
SW	[a]	50.27	78.38
WI	[a]	29.56	62.57
GWWI	[a]	41.83	72.65
GWSW	[a]	66.32	87.98
SWWI	[a]	34.08	66.63
GWSWWI	[a]	75.70	91.41
[b]	1	35.27	74.56
[b]	2	32.96	72.96
[b]	3	52.45	68.37

Notes
[a]For all samples pooled.
[b]All program responses pooled.

single and/or multi-component programs, the signs were correct but the differences were not significant.

Continuous WTP Data

Following the referendum question, respondents were asked an open-ended WTP question:

> Scientists cannot be certain about program costs: the final cost could be more or less than $xx. If you voted **Yes to the referendum question,** perhaps you would vote **for** the program at a higher cost. If you voted **No to {the referendum question}**, perhaps you would vote **Yes** at some lower cost or, perhaps the program would have to cost zero ($0) before you would vote for it. **What is the highest program cost at which you would vote Yes? Please write in your answer below.**

While the incentive properties of open-ended WTP follow-up questions are considered suspect, this data set nevertheless has the potential to cast light on three issues: the effect of referendum offer price on WTP (the 'starting point bias' issue), functional form for econometric analysis, and the relative magnitudes of mean and median WTP from referendum vs. continuous WTP data (conventional wisdom suggests the referendum data will generate larger WTP estimates).

Effect of referendum offer price

With the continuous WTP follow-up format, the referendum offer price serves as a starting price (SP) thereby permitting tests for SP influence on WTP. The literature yields many reports of significant SP effects (as well as reports of cases where no significant effects were found), and a variety of approaches to modeling SP effects. Boyle *et al.* (1985) assumed a simple linear model, $rWTP = \alpha + \beta SP$, where $rWTP$ is reported WTP, so that true $WTP = \alpha$, and any reported WTP beyond α is an artifact of SP. Farmer and Randall (1996) assume the respondent takes SP as providing some information, and ask how that information might affect a rational respondent's $rWTP$. They develop a number of response models, and suggest that the 'surplus preservation' model has conceptual appeal and some support from the empirical evidence. The surplus preservation model argues that respondents have a clear idea of their own WTP. In deciding what $rWTP$ to report, they are influenced by SPs below true WTP, which are taken as suggestions that the policy-maker might be willing to provide the program cheaply; so, respondents set $rWTP < WTP$ when $SP < WTP$. However, because there is no advantage in reporting $rWTP > WTP$, they are not influenced by $SP > WTP$. This model of respondent behavior predicts that $rWTP$ is positively correlated with SP for $SP < WTP$, but uncorrelated with SP for $SP \geq WTP$; graphically, $rWTP$ rises initially with

SP, but flattens as SP approaches WTP. The implication for interpreting rWTP is that, so long as the range of SPs used brackets WTP, rWTP reaches a maximum at WTP.

After deleting an additional set of responses with missing values for WTP, 318 response remained for analysis; of these, 86 reported WTP of zero. The Kruskal-Wallis nonparametric test for the influence of SP on rWTP (Table 5.4) shows that the hypothesis that SP has no influence on rWTP is rejected overwhelmingly for SP ={$10, 30, 54, 80, 120, 200}; on the other hand, for SP = {$54, 80, 120, 200} there was little evidence of any SP influence on rWTP. The hypothesis of linear response to SP is firmly rejected. Note also that the rWTP response to SP flattens as SP approaches 54, i.e., as it approaches the median rWTP. This empirical result is entirely consistent with the Farmer-Randall surplus preservation model of response, and can be interpreted as evidence that median rWTP is an unbiased estimator of median WTP.

Table 5.4. Kruskal-Wallis test for multiple independent samples, Ohio case study

Starting Price	# Obs	Median	Ave. Rank	Statistics H	Result	P-Value
$10	49	10.00	113.5			
30	64	30.00	137.3			
54	54	54.00	175.1			
80	96	50.00	181.7	24.95	Reject	0.0001
120	36	50.00	171.6			
200	19	50.00	173.7			
$54	54	54.00	97.9			
80	96	50.00	104.7		Fail to	
120	36	50.00	103.6	0.63	Reject	0.889
200	19	50.00	108.0			

Notes
H0: $\tau_1 = ... = \tau_k$
H1: τ.s are not all equal

Functional form
The literature displays some controversy as to whether zero-WTP observations should be treated as censored, so that true negative values are reported as zeros, or real. The functional form specified for econometric analysis should reflect what we believe about the underlying true

distribution of WTP. Proponents of treating WTP as censored argue that WTP is a censored metric of preference, because it does not permit expression of the differences in preference between zero-WTP respondents who are almost willing to pay a positive amount and those who are far from willing. Proponents of treating zero WTP observations as real argue that economic logic requires non-negative WTP for programs that would not reduce utility if implemented at no cost. We estimated continuous WTP models of both kinds, i.e., assuming WTP is censored and that zero-WTP observations are real. The basic model is WTP = f(P1, PP, ...), where WTP is a continuous variable; P1 = 1 if the referendum price is $10, and 0 otherwise ; PP = 1 if the referendum price is $54, $80, $120, or $200, and 0 otherwise; the omitted referendum price is $30; and the unlisted variables mirror those used in the probit analysis of referendum data (i.e., sociodemographic variables including income, use of the resources at issue, attitudinal variables, program dummies, and sample dummies).

For estimation, the OLS model is rejected as biased, given the prevalence of zero WTP responses. The tobit model assuming a censored normal distribution provided a poor, and arguably biased, fit of the data. The data, when plotted, look a lot like the log-normal and gamma distributions. These functional forms can be used in the tobit model, when the dependent variable is transformed to log (WTP + 1). The gamma distribution provided the more consistent and reasonable estimation results. In summary, of the models assuming the data are censored at zero, the tobit with gamma distribution was preferred. We then estimated the basic model with the gamma distribution, and assuming that zero-WTP observations are not censored but real. By standard econometric criteria, this model was preferred (slightly) to the tobit with gamma distribution model. Reported WTP (solid line) and the estimated WTP from the preferred (zeros-real, gamma distribution) model (dashed line) are plotted in Figure 5.3.

These econometric results provide some support for the approach of treating zero-WTP observations in continuous data sets as real, rather than censored observations.

Mean and median WTP: referendum vs. open-ended data
Conventional wisdom seems to have settled on the stylized fact that referendum data generate mean and median WTP estimates greater than those from continuous WTP, although it seems far from clear how much of this difference resides in the raw data and how much is an artifact of the functional forms used in econometric estimation.

As indicated above, the log-normal probit model provides a good fit within the range of the referendum data (which suggests good estimates of median WTP), but generates implausibly high estimates of mean WTP. The use of a lower bound mean calculated from the log-normal probit estimate reduces the extent of the problem. The gamma distribution provided the best fit of the continuous WTP data, but visual inspection suggests it tended to

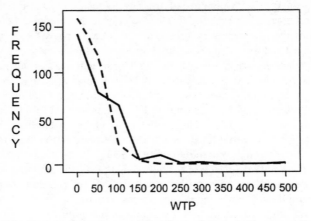

Figure 5.3. Density function, estimated wtp (zeros real, gamma), Ohio case study

understate mean WTP (Figure 5.3). There seems to be some support (Table 5.5) for the hypothesis that these two models bracket the true median and mean WTP. It is interesting to observe how closely median WTP from the referendum data coincides with mean WTP from the raw continuous data, as the Farmer-Randall surplus preservation model of starting price effects suggests.

Table 5.5. Median and Mean wtp($/household), all programs pooled, Ohio case study

	Median WTP	Mean WTP
Referendum, YNP data, log-normal	52	68 (LBM)
Continuous data, gamma distribution (zeros assumed real)	24	32
Continuous, raw data	25	47

Validity of Results
As is becoming all too common in research at academic institutions, this study was performed with a substantial investment in research design but inadequate funds for field data collection. The result was an elaborate split-sample research design supported by a relatively thin data set. The predictable outcome was that much of the statistical testing that would be *a*

priori desirable has been hampered or precluded in practice by inadequate sample size.

Nevertheless, there are some indications of validity. First, sound CV research practices have been followed. In particular: the split-sample design recommended by the NOAA panel (Arrow *et al.* 1993) was used; the questionnaires were carefully developed and pre-tested; and the programs offered were not merely plausible, in fact baseline conditions were realistic descriptions of actual conditions and with-program conditions were developed with the advice of knowledgeable policy-makers and scientists. Second, the multivariate probit analyses (Table 5.1) demonstrate construct validity. Third, the relationships among WTP for single and multi-component programs were mostly consistent with theoretical expectations as to sign, but significant in only one of six cases; this is a fairly strong result, given the split-sample design and the thin data set.

IMPLICATIONS AND CONCLUSIONS

Estimated median WTP provides a measure of the WTP of the median voting household, whereas LBM provides a lower-bound measure of mean benefits/household. The study generated estimates from two kinds of data sets, YN and YNP, and for three samples representing respectively the Maumee rural (MR), the Maumee urban (MU), and the Columbus-Cleveland (CC) populations. Obviously, some decisions about appropriate aggregation strategies must precede policy pronouncements.

First, we lean toward the LBM as a lower-bound estimate of mean WTP/household, the proper benefit measure for a potential Pareto-improvement test. Second, we lean toward the YNP data set for generating household-level WTP estimates, because there seemed insufficient reason to discard the rather large group of respondents who reported protest-no votes. So, benefit estimates reported below are one-time payments based on LBMs for YNP data, with zero WTP assigned to non-respondent households. Aggregation strategies require more subtle consideration; accordingly, we report results for more than one level of aggregation, and offer some commentary concerning aggregation levels.

Aggregating across the in-region population, MR + MU, the benefits of the GW program amount to $4.04 per acre of cropland. Adding-in the Columbus-Cleveland population generates a benefit estimate of $17.55 per acre. If one was willing to assume that WTP for the CC sample was representative of all households in non-Maumee-basin Ohio, an aggregate benefit of $71.02 would be obtained. Aggregating across just MR + MU populations ignores the strong evidence of positive out-of-region WTP. However, one wonders if out-of-region WTP for the GW program in the Maumee basin would have been so large if respondents were offered simultaneously GW programs in other cropland regions of the state.

Benefits of the surface water program, per acre of cropland, were $6.05 for MR + MU population, $26.06 for MR + MU + CC, and $101.30 for the population of Ohio. Given that sediments in the Maumee River eventually contaminate the western basin of Lake Erie, a popular resort area which draws visitors from much of Ohio and beyond, the broader aggregates have somewhat more credibility in the case of the SW program.

Benefits per acre of wetland to be protected amount to $1,077 for MR + MU population, $21,566 for MR + MU + CC, and $85,215 for the population of Ohio. These numbers may seem large, but the wetlands along the shore of the western basin of Lake Erie are a major resource that has already been much diminished, in close proximity to a popular resort area. We feel comfortable assuming a substantial clientele of active and passive users of this resource.

NOTE

1. Using the RHS variables defined below, we compared estimation results using four dependent variables: (1) Y=1, N=0; (2) P=1, N=0; (3) Y=1, P=0; and (4) Y=1, N or P = 0. Using criteria of goodness of fit, significance of dependent variables consistency across estimation equations, specification (2) was rejected: there was no justification for interpreting P votes as Y votes.

REFERENCES

Arrow, K., R. Solow, P. R. Portney, E. E. Leamer, R. Radner and H. Schuman (1993), 'Report of the NOAA panel on contingent valuation,' Resources for the Future, Washington DC.

Boyle, K.J., R.C. Bishop, and M.P. Welsh (1985), 'Starting point bias in contingent valuation bidding games,' *Land Economics,* 61:188-96.

Cooper, J.C. (1993), 'Optimal bid selection for dichotomous choice contingent valuation surveys,' *Journal of Environmental Economics and Management,* 24:25-40.

Diamond, P. (1996), 'Testing the internal consistency of contingent valuation,' *Journal of Environmental Economics and Management,* 30:337-47.

Dillman, Don A. (1978), *Mail and Telephone Surveys: The Total Design Method,* New York: Wiley.

Farmer, M.C., and A. Randall (1996), 'Referendum voting strategies and implications for follow-up open-ended responses,' *Benefits and Costs Transfer in Natural Resources Planning,* W-133, ninth interim report, pp. 263-95.

Haab, T. C. and K. E. McConnell (1997), 'Referendum models and negative willingness to pay: alternative solutions,' *Journal of Environmental Economics and Management,* 32:251-70.

Hoehn, J. P.   (1991), 'Valuing the multidimensional impacts of environmental policy: theory and methods,' *American Journal of Agricultural Economics*, **73**:289-99.

Hoehn, J. P. and J. B. Loomis (1993), 'Substitution effects in the valuation of multiple environmental programs,' *Journal of Environmental Economics and Management*, **25**:5-75.

Kahneman, D. and J. L. Knetsch (1992), 'Valuing public goods: the purchase of moral satisfaction,' *Journal of Environmental Economics and Management*, **22**:57-70.

Krosnick, J.A. (1991), 'Response strategies for coping with the cognitive demands of attitude measurement surveys,' *Applied Cognitive Psychology*, **5**:213-36.

Randall, A. and J. P. Hoehn (1996), 'Embedding in market demand systems,' *Journal of Environmental Economics and Management*, **30**:369-80.

6. Assessing the Accuracy of Benefits Transfers: Evidence From a Multi-Site Contingent Valuation Study of Ground Water Quality

Timothy P. VandenBerg, Gregory L. Poe, and John R. Powell

INTRODUCTION

Economists and policy analysts have long extolled the virtues of using cost-benefit analysis to weigh the usefulness of certain proposed government actions. Increasingly, this advice has been heeded. Every US president since 1975 has issued an Executive Order requiring federal agencies to prepare a cost-benefit analysis before promulgating major regulations.[1] And Congress, under the guise of regulatory reform, has frequently debated the merits of a statutory requirement that federal agencies prepare cost-benefit analyses for proposed and, in some instances, existing regulations.[2] The passage of such legislation appears increasingly likely as frustration grows with federal regulations that are perceived as cumbersome and costly (Congressional Green Sheets, 1998).

Preparing cost-benefit analyses that are comprehensive and capable of withstanding external scrutiny is time consuming and expensive (Congressional Budget Office, 1997). Despite this fact, agencies preparing cost-benefit analyses would be likely to work under severe time and cost constraints. Congress and the courts sometimes impose legally binding deadlines on agency rule-making (General Accounting Office, 1995). These deadlines can seriously limit the time available to satisfy cost-benefit analysis requirements. The annual discretionary appropriations that Congress makes available to fund federal agencies may also fail to keep pace with growing agency responsibilities and the demand for increasingly sophisticated economic analysis of regulations. In many instances time and cost constraints will preclude the conduct of primary research designed to provide input to cost-benefit analyses. This would be particularly true of primary research associated with non-market values, where defensible research is often quite time consuming and expensive.

The necessity for low cost and timely non-market valuation research has renewed academic and policy interest in transferring the findings of primary non-market valuation research conducted in one location to other locations, otherwise known as benefits transfer (Water Resources Research, 1992; Western Regional Research Project W-133, 1992; US Environmental Protection Agency, 1993; Downing and Ozuna, 1996; Kirchhoff *et al.* 1997; VandenBerg, 1995). While expert opinion, unit-day use values, and more formalized econometric techniques have long been used to transfer estimated resource values from original 'study' sites to unstudied 'policy' sites, there has been little systematic assessment of the accuracy of benefits transfers. Such a formal assessment is an essential first step for establishing when transfers should be conducted in lieu of original research, identifying strengths and weaknesses of the technique, and subsequently improving upon transfer use.

Using a multi-site contingent-valuation (CV) study of willingness to pay (WTP) for improvements in ground water quality, this chapter examines the relative accuracy of alternative benefits transfer methods. In contrast with previous studies of ground water quality that have transferred values across studies with different questionnaire formats, commodity definitions, population groups and policy issues (e.g., Crutchfield, 1994; Bergstrom and Boyle, 1993b), the data for this analysis was collected concurrently using the same CV questionnaire. As such, this study more closely approximates the ideal conditions for assessing the accuracy and validity of benefits transfers (Boyle and Bergstrom, 1992; McConnell, 1992) and tests of benefits transfer research employed for other environmental resources (Downing and Ozuna, 1996; Kirchhoff *et al.* 1997). The focus of this chapter differs however from past work, in that previous research has primarily focused on statistical analyses of benefits transfers from a single study site to another policy site. The intent of this chapter is to reorient the focus of benefits transfer research from the transfer of values across individual sites, to the use of pooled values from various study sites to provide the basis for benefits transfer and to improve the transferability of values. Also examined in this pooled approach is the relative accuracy of methods that transfer entire benefits functions and those that rely on the direct transfer of average values.

This chapter is organized as follows. The next section provides a conceptual framework and details the hypotheses to be tested. An overview of the CV study used as the basis for transfers is then provided, followed by an evaluation of the hypotheses identified in the second section, with the focus being on different groupings of study sites. The final section summarizes the findings and implications of this research.

CONCEPTUAL FRAMEWORK AND HYPOTHESES

As discussed in Chapter 1 (this book), the general conceptual model underlying ground water valuation research centers on the measurement of option prices for a risk change, and can be quite complex. For the purposes of this chapter, a simple characterization of WTP for ground water quality improvements for the ith individual at the jth site suffices, and is specified as

$$WTP_{ij} = \omega_j(Q_{ij}^0, Q_{ij}^1; I_{ij}, H_{ij}) \qquad (6.1)$$

where: ω_j is a functional specification of an average valuation function for the jth site; Q^0 and Q^1 are pre and post-improvement quality levels associated with a proposed project; I is income; and H represents a vector of other socio-economic characteristics.[3]

Following the benefits transfer nomenclature used by Desvousges *et al.* (1992) and others, the process of benefits transfer involves using prior research at a 'study' site (*s*), to provide information on values at a 'policy' site (*p*). The empirical policy question is whether estimated values 'transferred' from the study approximate the true value at the policy site, where the truth is taken to be the mean WTP value, $\overline{WTP_p}$, that would be estimated if an original study was conducted at the policy site. Transfer to the policy site may take one of two forms: as a 'direct' transfer of the mean WTP value obtained from the study site ($\overline{WTP_s} = \frac{1}{n_s}\sum_{i=1}^{n_s} WTP_{is}$) ; or as a transfer of the estimated 'benefit function' at the study site, $\hat{\omega}_s(.)$, to the policy site population characteristics,

(*i.e.* $\widehat{WTP}_{p|s} = \hat{\omega}_s(Q_p^0, Q_p^1; \bar{I}_p, \bar{H}_p))$. The prevailing presumption in the applied economics literature is that the transfer of the benefits function to the conditions at the policy site is preferred and more closely predicts $\overline{WTP_p}$ than the direct transfer (Loomis, 1992). The convergent validity between the transferred and the policy site values may be assessed in terms of statistical reliability, as has been the focus of recent papers by Downing and Ozuna (1996) and Kirchhoff *et al.* (1997). It may also take the form of percentage error, as examined in Loomis (1992) and Kirchhoff *et al.* (1997).

As tests of convergent validity, and the relative merits of the direct and benefits function transfer approaches, the following hypotheses will be examined:

$$H_0^1: \overline{WTP_s} = \overline{WTP_p}, \tag{6.2a}$$

$$H_0^2: \hat{WTP}_{p|s} = \overline{WTP_p}, \text{ and} \tag{6.2b}$$

$$H_0^3: \left| \frac{\overline{WTP_s} - \overline{WTP_p}}{\overline{WTP_p}} \right| \geq \left| \frac{\hat{WTP}_{p|s} - \overline{WTP_p}}{\overline{WTP_p}} \right| \tag{6.2c}$$

Corresponding with the direct transfer, H_0^1 is a simple test of equality between the mean values from the study and policy sites. This takes the form of a t-test in a simple one-to-one transfer case, and an F-test when multiple sites are considered. Following Kirchhoff *et al.* (1997), a second statistical approach is to evaluate whether the mean WTP from the study site lies in the 90 percent confidence interval ($CI^{0.90}$) of the estimated value at the policy site, i.e., $\overline{WTP_s} \in CI_p^{0.90}$.[4] While the difference of means test corresponds more closely with standard methods of comparing samples, the latter test may be more policy relevant in the sense that it asks whether the best estimate from the study site would lie in the range of what could be obtained by a new study at the policy site. This latter approach is also more restrictive in the sense that it only accounts for the variance of the policy site variables.

Similarly, two separate tests are associated with H_0^2. First, a pooled regression Chow test approach is used to test the statistical similarity of the benefits functions at the study and policy sites. Such a test poses the fundamental empirical question of whether benefits functions are universal across sites, as opposed to the more simplistic assumption of invariant average values associated with H_0^1. In parallel with the first hypothesis, an alternative statistical test of accuracy is whether the predicted values using the study site benefits function in conjunction with sample characteristics from the policy site fall within the confidence interval at the policy site, i.e., $\hat{WTP}_{p|s} \in CI_p^{0.90}$.

As shown in the previous chapters and Chapter 8 of this book, ground water CV studies have reported a wide range of annual average WTP values, suggesting that H_1^0 will be rejected in most cases given the current body of research. Yet, in meta analyses of these studies Boyle *et al.* (1994) found evidence of systematic variation in WTP values across study site characteristics, lending some *a priori* hope that equality of benefits functions may hold.[5] To date, however, the convergent validity of direct and benefit function transfer methods has not been addressed using study and policy site data for drinking water quality.[6]

Both H_0^1 and H_0^2 have statistical connotations. However, it is important to recognize that statistical criteria associated with hypothesis tests may not correspond to acceptable notions of accuracy in a policy context. The variance, and hence the range of the confidence intervals surrounding the mean WTP estimates, may be large or small, and are largely driven by sample size. For example, transfers may exhibit small percentage errors but still be significantly different. This is the case in the Downing and Ozuna (1996) paper, in which an estimated mean WTP value of $85.91 would have been judged to be statistically different from an estimated value of $79.42 using a non-overlapping confidence intervals criterion. Whether an 8 percent difference in values is policy relevant is an open question. Conversely, if the confidence intervals are wide, a transfer of values may have a large percentage error but not be significantly different.

From a policy perspective, the accuracy (or inaccuracy) of the estimate may be a more relevant parameter. H_0^3 examines the relative accuracy of the direct and benefits function transfer approaches, i.e., testing whether the benefit function transfer approach is more accurate than the direct transfer. Emphasis in this analysis is given to visual inspection of the mean and range of values. A Wilcoxon Signed-Rank test is used to statistically compare the accuracy of matched direct and benefit function transfers at various points in this analysis.

DATA

Data for this analysis is taken from a CV study of ground water quality reported in detail in Powell (1991), and Powell *et al.* (1994). The objective of Powell's original study was to measure contingent values in individual towns, and to investigate how these values might influence local decision-making on ground water protection issues (see Powell *et al.* 1994). Although not created for benefits transfer research, the multi-site study design offers a unique opportunity for assessing the three stated hypotheses and the relative accuracy of transfers.

The design of the Powell (1991) survey was predicated on both conceptual and practical factors. Contingent valuation questionnaires were sent concurrently to households in 12 towns, four each in Massachusetts, Pennsylvania, and New York. These states were chosen because many cases of public water supply contamination had been reported in all three states, and the approach of each state government to controlling ground water contamination differed. Individual towns in the study were selected on the basis of population size (<20,000), reliance on ground water for water supply, and history of ground water contamination. Six of the 12 towns were selected because they had experienced contamination of their water supplies by Trichlorethylene (TCE) within the previous ten years. The six other towns, thought not to have experienced any contamination, were then chosen to serve as a control group.[7]

The survey was conducted in 1989. A total of 2,102 surveys were sent out to addresses from a systematic random sample of local tax rolls. Each member of the sample was contacted up to four times (two mailings of the survey each followed by reminder letters). Overall the response rate to the initial survey was 51.2% (n=1,041), after correcting for 67 undeliverable surveys.[8]

The sample used in this benefit transfer analysis is substantially lower than the number of returned surveys (1,041). First, 187 respondents using private wells were removed from the usable survey pool. This was done because in the Powell (1991) regressions, private well users and public supply users had significantly different responses to several important survey questions (e.g., future contamination, sources of contamination), and a dummy variable for private well users in a WTP regression of all respondents had a value of $14.04 that differed significantly from zero at $\alpha=10$ percent. Moreover, it is questionable whether public and private users value the same commodity: private well owners do not pay water bills, are not protected by drinking water standards, may have a more intimate knowledge of their water supply, and cannot call on their municipal water supplier should their water supply become unpotable. A number of surveys were also dropped from the sample because of item non-response, which precludes inclusion of entire observations for statistical analyses. As is typical of survey research, some respondents were hesitant to reveal information regarding their income. Of surveys received from public water users, 94 respondents chose not to reveal their income level. Additional observations were also rendered unusable for the analysis due to item non-response scattered among various questions.

The CV scenario used to elicit WTP values was developed over three pages. The first page presented respondents with pen-and-ink sketches of common sources of ground water contamination and asked which ones they were most concerned about. The second page elicited current ground water safety perceptions, with choices consisting of a four-level safety scale, including UNSAFE, SOMEWHAT SAFE, SAFE, VERY SAFE, accompanied by a verbal description. This safety-based format offers a unique approach to ground water valuation, and contrasts with more widely used subjective and objective assessments of exceeding standards that follow the approach developed initially in Edwards (1988). On the third page respondents were presented with a hypothetical scenario which queried them for their WTP to increase their water safety level to a 'VERY SAFE' level using a payment card format. The specific policy proposed to attain this safety level was 'the establishment of an area wide special water protection district.' In addition, following standard CV protocol, respondents were asked a number of background and commodity perception questions prior to the CV question, and demographic and other questions at the conclusion of the survey.

Table 6.1 shows that WTP, socioeconomic characteristics, and perceptions varied across towns. As examined extensively in Powell (1991), these socioeconomic characteristics and perceptions vary widely within sites, across individual sites, and across previous contamination experience and state groupings.

An OLS regression was estimated for the entire set of observations.[9] As depicted in Table 6.2, the sign of the coefficients corresponds to prior expectations, using variables and expectations identified in previous ground water research (VandenBerg, 1995). This regression indicates that WTP generally increases with subjective perceptions of past contamination, number of contamination sources, likelihood of future contamination, interest in community issues and perceptions that water sources were NOT SAFE. Respondents with higher incomes and education have higher WTP values on average, as do respondents who have a greater aversion to voluntary risks and a greater trust in ability to protect public water supplies. Although the model has a low R^2 value of 15%, this value falls within the range of other ground water CV studies of public water users that might be used for benefits transfers (e.g., 6.8% in McClelland *et al.*, 1992; 11 to 14% in Jordan and Elnagheeb, 1993). In addition, the overall model was significant ($p < 0.01$), and the individual covariates also had high levels of significance. For those covariates in Table 6.2 that are not significant at standard levels, the individual coefficients and/or the group of coefficients have significance levels of $p=0.15$ or better.

RESULTS

Benefits Transfers Across Individual and All Town Study Sites

Given the diversity in WTP and socioeconomic characteristics across towns, there are several possible subgroups of similar towns that might be considered for the assessment of benefits transfers. This section evaluates the hypotheses and relative accuracy for the two most extreme cases: transfers of mean WTP values using individual towns as study and policy sites; and transfers using study site mean WTP values computed for all but one town which subsequently serves as the policy site (respectively referred to as the n-1 and nth values). The former approach corresponds with crude scoping studies that attempt to develop 'ball park' estimates of potential benefits at policy sites (Bergstrom and Boyle, 1993a). It is also the practice evaluated in the Kirchhoff *et al.* (1997) and the Downing and Ozuna (1996) papers. The latter, n-1 to nth transfer approach, follows a 'data splitting' approach (Meyers, 1986) that approximates the protocol of forming values transferable from several study sites. This technique was used in Loomis (1992). A summary of these comparisons is found in the first two columns of Table 6.3, and transferred values for each group of sites is reported in VandenBerg (1995). The 'state' and 'contam.' data in the last two columns are discussed in the next section.

The relative accuracy of direct and benefit function transfers for study sites based on individual and n-1 town groupings is depicted in the first two rows of

Table 6.3. Transfers of individual town WTP values for direct and benefit function transfers have average accuracies of 42.1% and 44.1% respectively. These were not statistically different using a Wilcoxon ranked-sum test (p=0.70). When study sites are pooled across 11 towns for transfer to the 12th town, there is an improvement in the accuracy of both the direct and benefit function approaches. This improvement in accuracy is most dramatic for the benefit function approach, for which the average error fell to 18.3%. Similar trends are noted for the maximum observed error, which fell considerably for both direct and benefit function transfers as demonstrated in the range of errors in Table 6.3. Now we turn to the statistical hypotheses.

Examination of hypothesis H_0^1 for individual town transfers rejects equality of mean WTP values in 30 (or 45.5%) of the 66 possible pairwise comparisons at α=10%, using a standard difference of means test. Using a similar test, comparisons of n-1 mean WTP values to nth town mean WTP values result in rejections of equality in 4 (or 33.3%) of the 12 possible tests. The test, $\overline{WTP}_s \in CI_p^{0.90}$, provided like results, with 55.3% of the individual transfers and 33.3% of the n-1 transfers falling outside $CI_p^{0.90}$, a notable improvement. The observed decline in rejection proportion between the individual and the n-1 approach is attributed to the greater study site variation of hypothetical sample sites, consisting of the aggregated values from 11 towns.

Hypothesis H_0^2 was examined using a Chow test for model equality to statistically compare study and policy site benefit functions. Across individual towns the hypothesis of benefit function equality, H_0^2, was rejected in 24 (or 36.4%) of the 66 comparisons. Rejection of H_0^2 occurred in 4 (or 25%) of the 12 tests using the n-1 approach. These results suggest that variations in average WTP values between towns may not simply be attributed to differences in population distributions or differences in survey design. However, the majority of cases do support H_0^2 and the theoretical rationale for function-based transfers.

The second test of H_0^2 which focused on $\overline{WTP}_{p|s} \in CI_p^{0.90}$ showed similar improvements associated with grouping. Of the individual transfers, 56.8% of the transferred values fell outside the 90% CI of the study site. When n-1 study sites were grouped, this value fell to 16.7%. Thus, it appears that there is substantial improvement in predictive power associated with grouping.

The results of H_0^3 are also affected by grouping, as indicated in the last row of Table 6.3. For the individual transfers, slightly less than half of the time the error associated with benefits function transfers is lower than the error associated with direct transfers. As noted above, these two methods do not provide significantly different distributions of errors for the individual transfers. When the n-1 sample approach is used, the prediction error associated with benefit function transfers is smaller than direct function

Table 6.1. Descriptive statistics by town, MA, PA and NY benefits transfer study

State Town	WTP ($)	Std. Err. WTP ($)	Obs.	Prev. Cont. (TCE)	Perc. Hist. Cont.	Likeli-hood of Future Cont.	Water Safety	Interest	Avg. Risk	Number of Cont. Sources	Avg. Trust	% College Educated	Income ($1,000)
Massachusetts													
Westford	71.54	11.89	47	0	1.30	2.38	2.62	2.98	4.06	3.45	1.86	46.4	45.9
Groveland	108.49	16.76	48	1	2.40	2.58	2.46	3.33	4.05	3.31	1.96	40.4	37.8
Rowly	79.45	11.72	50	1	1.90	2.84	2.50	3.14	4.04	3.12	1.76	49.1	41.3
Salisbury	74.07	13.33	51	0	1.31	2.98	3.52	2.84	4.03	3.37	1.72	22.4	32.8
Pennsylvania													
Chalfont	61.71	9.10	57	0	1.19	2.39	2.68	2.82	4.06	3.35	1.87	34.2	43.2
Perkassie	48.69	10.33	61	1	1.49	2.66	2.57	2.89	3.97	3.28	1.94	35.1	29.7
Horsham	67.45	12.10	46	1	1.24	2.63	2.54	2.63	4.00	3.17	1.91	48.2	45.5
E. Greenville	65.00	9.83	38	0	1.18	2.61	2.60	2.87	4.11	3.02	1.91	16.7	27.2

State Town	WTP ($)	Std. Err. WTP ($)	Obs.	Prev. Cont. (TCE)	Perc. Hist. Cont.	Likeli-hood of Future Cont.	Water Safety	Interest	Avg. Risk	Number of Cont. Sources	Avg. Trust	% College Educated	Income ($1,000)
New York													
Olean	41.19	7.89	70	1	1.31	2.59	2.63	2.77	3.87	3.46	1.90	19.3	28.7
Salamanca	31.96	6.98	68	0	1.97	1.97	3.04	2.91	3.75	2.99	1.99	18.9	21.5
Bath	42.44	9.04	42	0	1.26	1.95	2.98	2.69	3.96	2.81	2.09	34.8	27.4
Macedon	74.87	13.43	39	1	1.56	2.74	2.54	2.77	3.92	3.79	2.08	25.6	30.4

Notes:

WTP: willingness to pay for additional ground water protection, $/Household/Year.

Prev. Cont.: binary variable indicating towns that had experienced past ground water contamination by Trichloroethylene(TCE).

Perc. Hist. Cont.: categorical response variable for perception of previous pollution of household drinking water: 1= No Cont, 2= Don't Know,

3 = Yes Cont.

Likelihood of Future Cont.: five point scale response to likelihood of future contamination ranging from very unlikely to very likely.

Water Safety: four point categorical response to current safety question.

Interest: four point scale response to how interested respondent is in drinking water quality in the community.

Avg. risk: Voluntary risk perception variable, mean of three categorical questions with answers ranging from 1=unsafe to 5=very safe.

Number of Cont. Sources: Number of perceived potential contamination sources, out of six possible.

Avg. Trust: Composite variable of respondents' trust in government and scientific organizations, an average of 9 questions: answers ranging from

Table 6.2. *OLS regression estimates of WTP model for ground water protection, entire data set, MA, PA and NY benefits transfer study*

Variable	Sign Expectation	Coefficient (Standard Error)
Intercept		-29.68 (30.66)
Perception of Contamination: have not had a previous contamination experience.[a]	-	-23.48 (8.10)[f]
Perception of Contamination: don't know if had a previous contamination experience[a]	-	-26.96 (11.30)[g]
Likelihood of future contamination: likely or very likely[b]	+	17.51 (10.95)
Likelihood of future contamination: not sure[b]	+	9.41 (7.56)
Interest: mild or no interest in community water issues[c]	-	-20.66 (8.53)[g]
Interest: interested in community water issues[c]	-	-11.15 (7.72)
Safety: current water quality perception, unsafe or somewhat safe[d]	+	29.92 (12.82)[g]
Safety: current water quality perception, safe[d]	0	21.07 (11.68)[h]
Education: college degree[e]	?	17.51 (8.42)[g]
Education: some college[e]	?	15.72 (7.74)[g]

Variable	Sign Expectation	Coefficient (Standard Error)
Risk Perceptions: average of three questions with 5 point responses ranging from 1=extremely safe to 5=extremely unsafe.	+	9.91 (5.87)[h]
Sources: number of perceived potential contamination sources	+	2.56 (1.74)
Trust: average of nine questions of respondent trust in government and scientific organization ranging from 1 = do not trust to 3 = great trust.	+	15.67 (6.92)[g]
I: Household Income ($/year) based on the midpoint of the reported income interval	0	0.0008 (0.00017)[f]
F Statistic		7.51[f]
R-Square		0.15
n		617

Notes
Baseline for binary variables
[a] indicated a contamination experience,
[b]very unlikely or unlikely to have a contamination experience,
[c]strong interest in community issues,
[d]very safe current perceived water safety level,
[e]high school or less.
[f]significance at the 1 percent level.
[g]significance at the 5 percent level.
[h]significant at the 10 percent level.
Source: VandenBerg, 1995

The economic value of water quality

Table 6.3. Measures of accuracy using policy site as base, various data Subgroupings, MA, PA and NY benefits transfer study

	Ind. to Ind. (n=132)	All n-1 (n=12)	State n-1 (n=4)	Contam. n-1 (n=6)
Mean Direct Error (DE) % (Range) in Relative Accuracy %	42.1 (1.1, 239.4)	31.4 (0.2, 105.0)	21.8 (3.29, 57.0)	35.5 (3.06, 100.1)
Mean Benefit Function. Error (BFE) % (Range) in Relative Accuracy %	44.1 (0.4, 297.6)	18.3 (0.8, 55.6)	19.1 (0.2, 38.7)	15.5 (2.1, 50.4)
H_0^1: % Reject Difference of Means at 10% Level	45.5	33.3	25.0	41.7
H_0^1: % where $\overline{WTP}_s \notin CI_P^{0.90}$	55.3	33.3	25.0	41.7
H_0^2: % Reject Chow Equality Across Functions at 10% Level	36.4	25.0	25.0	16.7
H_0^2: % where $\widehat{WTP}_{p|s} \notin CI_P^{0.90}$	56.8	16.7	16.7	16.7
H_0^3: % BFE < DE (Wilcoxon rank-sum test)	48.5 (p=0.69)	75.0 (p=0.03)	66.7 (p=0.64)	91.7 (p=0.01)

transfers 75% of the time. In this instance, the differences are judged to be statistically significantly different (p=0.03).

Thus it appears that the construction of study sites used to conduct transfers has a distinct impact on the accuracy of value estimates. Aggregating several towns to form study sites improves the accuracy of benefit function transfers and, to a lesser extent, direct transfers. Importantly, from a safety-first perspective (where importance is placed on avoiding large errors), maximum errors in the n-1 approach were substantially lower than those associated with individual transfers. As such it appears that the increased variation associated with pooling diverse towns is more than offset by the additional n associated with larger samples. We explore this issue further in the following sections.

Transfers Within Alternative Study Site Town Groups
In practice, benefits transfers do not typically use all available study sites. Nor do they rely on a single site. Applying prior information and judgement, researchers frequently group particular study sites into like categories for assimilation into the analysis, while omitting other sites (e.g., Desvousges, *et al.* 1992; Loomis, 1992; Boyle and Bergstrom, 1992). This section examines the effect of alternative town groupings on the accuracy of benefits transfers, using the n-1 data splitting technique as the basis for comparisons.

Two groupings of like towns were identified following the primary study design: categorization by state and contamination history. Each state has different local government, outreach, and regulatory structures relative to ground water protection. It was also hypothesized that prior experience with contamination would affect stated WTP. The predictive accuracy for these two groupings is summarized in the last two columns of Table 6.3.

When grouped by state, direct transfer errors improved to 21.8%, and the average benefit function transfer error fell to 19.1%. Two factors appear to contribute to this reduction in error. First, there is an 'aggregation' effect associated with merging multiple towns into a single study site, and second there are 'grouping' effects from organizing towns into like groups. To isolate these effects, 100 random combinations of four towns, taken without replacement from all 12, were used to compute overall average direct and benefit function prediction errors. These provided errors of 35.0% and 21.6% respectively, using the n-1 sample method (see Table 6.4). Comparing the actual within-state results with these average random grouping errors suggests that aggregation effects have a large impact on benefit function accuracies, while the like town or grouping effect is more dominant for direct transfers. This appears to be due to the fact that WTP values vary significantly across states (F=12.45, p < 0.0; average WTP for Massachusetts ($83.87), Pennsylvania ($59.79) and New York ($44.56)).

When towns were grouped instead by previous contamination experience, the accuracy of benefit function and direct approaches diverged. Relative to the prior subgroupings, direct transfer accuracy worsened with average predictive errors of 35.5%. In contrast, benefit function accuracy improved with average errors of 15.5%. As shown in Table 6.3, this divergence is further reflected in the frequency that direct transfer errors were lower than that of benefit function transfers. As noted previously, this result is associated with both aggregation and grouping effects. Here, the primary gains from direct transfers are associated with aggregation effects, as demonstrated in Table 6.4. Indeed, the actual grouping is less accurate on average than a random selection of towns, an observation that is probably owing to the lack of variation in values across groups. While a comparison of the means of the contaminated ($66.74) and uncontaminated towns ($56.94) has the expected direction, these values are not significantly different (F=2.27, p=0.13). In contrast, both an aggregation and grouping effect are observed for the benefit function transfer.

As indicated in Table 6.3, these diverging directions in accuracy correspond with the proportion of rejections of H_0^1 and H_0^2. State level grouping leads to a similar reduction in H_0^1 and H_0^2 rejections relative to the individual transfers. Reflecting these results, both direct and benefit function transfers demonstrated increased accuracy relative to individual transfers. However, when the grouping was arranged in a way that the rejection of the two hypotheses diverged, as occurred in the grouping by previous contamination experience, then so to did the effects on H_3^0. This issue is explored in greater detail in the next section.

Table 6.4. Accuracy improvements due to sample size for direct and benefits function transfers, MA, PA and NY benefits transfer study

Direct transfers	Data Grouping	
	State	Contamination
Random Grouping[a]	35.0	33.0
Actual Grouping	21.8	35.5
Improvement over Random	13.1	-2.5
Benefit Function Transfers		
Random Grouping[a]	21.6	20.1
Actual Grouping	19.1	15.5
Improvement over Random	2.6	4.6

Notes:
[a]Random grouping based on 100 random combinations of four towns (for the State grouping) and six towns (for the Contamination grouping) taken without replacement from all 12.

Correspondence between H_0^1 and H_0^2 Tests and Predictive Results

To this point, the analysis of H_0^3 has focused on hypothesis tests across all possible transfers, without distinguishing between transfers by the results of H_0^1 and H_0^2. *A priori*, we might expect different levels of accuracy associated with the acceptance or rejection of these hypothesis tests. For example, it is reasonable to presume that WTP predications for the policy sites, based on study site models that are statistically different, *i.e.* $\hat{WTP}_p \neq \hat{WTP}_s$, would be liable to more erroneous predictions than cases in which the estimated functions are equal. Adopting this logic, Loomis (1992) used functional inequality as a rationale for not conducting interstate transfers of demand functions between states where functional equality did not hold. The conjecture that functional inequality will prompt inaccurate transfers is examined here using Chow test results in conjunction with measures of predictive accuracies. In Table 6.5 each of the simulated transfer groupings are divided between sites which passed H_0^2.

Table 6.5. Average percentage errors and benefit function equivalence, MA, PA, and NY benefits transfer study

Data Subdivision	Transfer Type	Average Percentage Error	
		Do Not Reject H_0^2	Reject H_0^2
Individual Town	Benefit Function	35.8	53.8
	Direct	33.0	48.7
		(n=76)	(n=56)
All Data	Benefit Function	18.5	17.8
	Direct	33.1	26.5
		(n=9)	(n=3)
By State	Benefit Function	16.6	26.5
	Direct	18.4	32.3
		(n=9)	(n=3)
By Contamination	Benefit Function	13.6	25.0
Experience	Direct	35.3	36.6
		(n=9)	(n=2)

Note
Rejection of H_0^2 corresponds to the equality of functions Chow test criteria.

This appraisal of transfer accuracy based on demand function equality, or inequality, is hampered by the small number of transfers for 'all data', 'by state', and 'by contamination experience' subdivisions. Nonetheless a brief review of the results is useful. Average predictive error for the 'all data', 'by state', and 'by contamination experience' subdivisions where functional equality holds, indicates that transfers between sites with similar demand functions lead to predictions with smaller prediction errors than do direct value transfers. In a surprising result, individual town functional transfers in both functional equality cases were exceeded in accuracy by direct transfers, though not by a large amount.

Further examination of this result indicates it may be driven by the relationships between H_0^1 and H_0^2. As indicated in Table 6.6, in cases where H_0^1 is rejected and H_0^2 is not, we would expect the benefit function to provide better results. The opposite result occurs when H_0^1 is not rejected, but H_0^2 is rejected. Not surprisingly, when both H_0^1 and H_0^2 are rejected predictive errors for both value and function transfers are large. And when neither H_0^1 nor H_0^2 are rejected, predicted errors are relatively small. However, as is evident from the previous discussion, caution should be taken about drawing too many conclusions from individual transfers.

Table 6.6. Average percentage errors for individual town transfers for H_0^1 and H_0^2, MA, PA and NY benefits transfer study

	Transfer Type	Do Not Reject H_0^2	Reject H_0^2
Do Not Reject H_0^1	Benefit Function	30.1	36.8
	Direct	19.4	21.8
		(n=50)	(n=32)
Reject H_0^1	Benefit Function	48.1	76.5
	Direct	62.5	84.5
		(n=26)	(n=24)

Note
Rejection of H_0^2 corresponds to the equality of functions Chow test criteria, while rejection of H_0^1 corresponds with the equality of means t-test criteria.

IMPLICATIONS AND CONCLUSIONS

Clearly study site town aggregation plays an important role in the relative accuracy of transfers, a point that benefit transfer practitioners need to recognize in future research. When examined from the perspective of individual site-to-site transfers, this study provides results that reflect conclusions reached in previous benefits transfer research on other environmental resources. On average, benefit function transfers and direct transfers are not particularly accurate, with an average error range of 42% to 44% and maximum observed errors as high as 239% to 298%. This finding is reflected by a high rate of rejection in statistical comparisons of actual WTP values and WTP values predicted using study site benefit functions. Also, the distribution of transfer errors is not significantly different between benefits function and direct transfers. On the basis of these findings alone, this research would seem to support the conclusions reached by previous researchers that neither the direct nor benefits function transfer approaches are reliable approaches for estimating the values at a policy site.

However, based on our experimentation with alternative groupings of data to form study sites, we retain some optimism about the reliable use of benefits transfers. In all cases in which sites were grouped in meaningful ways, there was an improvement in the statistical reliability and the accuracy of the transfer. This improvement results from two sources. First, there is a simple aggregation effect associated with increasing the number of observations as well as the range of situations covered by the study site. Second, there is a like grouping effect associated with groupings that are correlated with WTP values. The former effect is particularly prominent for benefits function transfers, while the latter exerts the greatest effect on direct value transfers. Alternative groupings for transfers are shown in this data to reduce average errors of benefit function transfers by as much as two-thirds, and direct transfers by as much as one-half. Similar, but slightly more pronounced, effects on maximum observed errors are noted. Yet a determination regarding whether these average levels of transfers errors associated with the best groupings (which ranged between 16 and 22 percent) are 'acceptable' remains an area for policy discussion.

A second lesson from this analysis is that, except for the case of the individual site to site transfers, benefit function transfers tend to dominate direct transfers in terms of accuracy. This relative improvement is particularly significant in study site groupings that are formed from data (such as all study sites and by previous contamination) that are not highly correlated with WTP, and appears to be associated with greater variability in both the dependent and independent variables.

NOTES

1. Executive Order No. 12866, signed by President Clinton, is a recent order requiring federal agencies to perform cost-benefit analysis.
2. Examples of such legislation include H.R. 9 in the 104th Congress and S. 981 in the 105th Congress.
3. This simplified presentation assumes that prices, including water prices of alternative sources, are constant. This assumption is made, in part, because of lack of such information for each of the study sites.
4. Because our research focuses on alternative groupings of study sites with which to conduct transfers, and hence varies with the number of observations included at the study sites, the reverse comparison suggested in Kirchkoff *et al.* (1997) of whether $\overline{WTP}_p \in CI_S^{0.90}$ is not conducted because $CI_s^{0.90}$ is a moving target highly dependent on the sample size of the pooled group.

5. This conclusion is supported by the application of a proposed value function methodology to ground water quality studies, which found that predicted values for policy sites deviated from actual values and can be attributed to inconsistent definitions of ground water contaminants, explanatory variables and policy issues in the individual studies (Bergstrom and Boyle, 1993a, 1993b).
6. In an evaluation of travel cost of sport fishing, Loomis (1992) found that the benefit function generally performs better than direct transfers when H_2^0 is not rejected.
7. However, one of these towns, Salamanca New York, was later found to have had experienced contamination of its water supply by diesel fuel oil.
8. The overall response rate for the Powell survey places it in the middle of other ground water contingent valuation studies, whose rates varied from 35% (Jordan and Elnagheeb, 1993) to 78% (Poe,1993).
9. Alternative maximum likelihood modeling approaches were considered such as the Tobit (e.g. see Chapter 4 of this book) or a bounded likelihood model (e.g., Cameron and Huppert, 1989). While such models are desirable in the sense that they avoid truncation bias associated with zero dollar observations, which is a noted problem with OLS estimation, the maximum likelihood approach generally requires larger sample sizes than provided in some of the individual town data used here. Thus, OLS estimates were used for the statistical tests.

REFERENCES

Bergstrom, J. C. and K. J. Boyle (1993a), 'Using benefits transfer to value groundwater benefits: conceptual issues,' Discussion Paper Prepared for joint AAEA/AERE meetings Orlando, Florida, August.

Bergstrom, J. C. and K. J. Boyle (1993b), 'Benefit transfer case study: benefits of groundwater protection in Dougherty County, Georgia,' paper prepared for AERE workshop on Benefit transfer, Snowbird, UT. In: *Benefits Transfer: Procedures, Problems, and Research Needs*. US EPA #230-R-93-018.

Boyle, K. J. and J. C. Bergstrom (1992), 'Benefits transfer studies: myths, pragmatism, and idealism,' *Water Resources Research* **28**(3):657-63.

Boyle, K. J., G. L. Poe, and J. C. Bergstrom (1994), 'What do we know about groundwater values? Preliminary implications from a meta analysis of contingent-valuation studies,' *American Journal of Agricultural Economics*, **76**(5): 1055-61.

Cameron, T.A. and D.D. Huppert (1989), 'OLS versus ML estimation of non-market resource values with payment card interval data,' *Journal of Environmental Economics and Management,* **17**(3):230-46.

Congressional Budget Office (1997), 'Regulatory impact analyses: costs at selected agencies and implications for the legislative process,' Congressional Budget Office Papers.

Congressional Green Sheets (1998), 'Environment and energy special report, August 11, 1998.'

Crutchfield, S. R. (1994), 'Estimating the value of ground water protection: an application of benefits transfer,' a paper prepared for the Annual meetings of the American Agricultural Economics Association, San Diego, CA, August.

Desvousges, W. H., M. C. Naughton, and G. R. Parsons (1992), 'Benefits transfer: conceptual problems in estimating water quality benefits using existing studies,' *Water Resources Research*, **28**(3):675-83.

Downing, M, and T. Ozuna Jr. (1996), 'Testing the reliability of the benefit function transfer approach,' *Journal of Environmental Economics and Management*, **30**(3): 316-22.

Edwards, S. F. (1988), 'Option prices for groundwater protection,' *Journal of Environmental Economics and Management*, **15**:465-87.

General Accounting Office (1995), 'Regulatory reform: information on costs, cost effectiveness, and mandated deadlines for regulations,' Briefing Report to the Ranking Minority Member, Committee on Governmental Affairs, US Senate. (GAO/PEMD-95-18BR).

Kirchhoff, S., B. G. Colby, and J. T. LaFrance (1997), 'Evaluating the performance of benefit transfer: an empirical inquiry,' *Journal of Environmental Economics and Management*, **33**(1):75-93.

Jordan, J. L. and A. H. Elnagheeb (1993), 'Willingness to pay for improvements in drinking water quality,' *Water Resources Research*, **29**(2):237-45.

Loomis, J. B. (1992), 'The evaluation of a more rigorous approach to benefit transfer: benefit function transfer,' *Water Resources Research*, **28**(3):701-705.

McClelland, G. H., W. D. Schulze, J. K. Lazo, D. M. Waldman, J. K. Doyle, S. R. Elliott, and J. R. Irwin (1992), *Methods for Measuring Non-Use Values: A Contingent Valuation Study of Ground Water Cleanup, Final Report*, Office of Policy, Planning and Evaluation, US Environmental Protection Agency, Cooperative Agreement #CR-815183.

McConnell, K.E. (1992), 'Model building and judgment: implications for benefit transfer with travel cost models,' *Water Resources Research* **28**(3):695-700.

Meyers, R. (1986), *Classical and Modern Regression with Applications*, Duxbury Press, Boston, MA.

Poe, G. L. (1993), *Information, Risk Perceptions, and Contingent Values: The Case of Nitrates in Groundwater*, Unpublished Ph.D. dissertation, University of Wisconsin, Madison, WI.

Powell, J. R. (1991), *The Value of Groundwater Protection: Measurement of Willingness-To-Pay information and Its Utilization by Local Government Decision-Makers*, Unpublished Ph.D. Dissertation, Cornell University, Ithaca, NY.

Powell, J. R., D. J. Allee and C. McClintock (1994), 'Groundwater protection benefits and local community planning: impact of contingent valuation information,' *American Journal of Agricultural Economics*, **76**(5): 1061-75.

US Environmental Protection Agency (1993), *Benefits Transfer: Procedures, Problems, and Research Needs,* US EPA #230-R-93-018. AERE workshop on Benefit Transfer, Snowbird, UT.

VandenBerg, T.P. (1995), *Assessing the Accuracy of Benefits Transfers: Evidence from a Multi-Site Contingent Valuation Study of Groundwater Quality,* Unpublished Masters Thesis, Cornell University, Ithaca, NY.

Water Resources Research, Special Section (1992), 'Problems and issues in the validity of benefits transfer methodologies,' *Water Resources Research,* **28**(3):651-722.

Western Regional Research Project W-133 (1992), Benefits and Costs Transfer in Natural Resource Planning: Proposal For Revision, 1992-1997.

7. Benefits Transfer: The Case of Nitrate Contamination in Pennsylvania, Georgia and Maine

Willard Delavan and Donald J. Epp

INTRODUCTION

Benefits transfer is the practice of using benefits estimates from one or more existing studies to value changes in a similar good or service in a different time or place in lieu of directly estimating the benefits. This practice reduces research costs (Kask and Shogren, 1994) as well as potentially reducing the time it takes policy makers to make informed decisions (Bingham, 1992).

In addition to cost savings there are several reasons why benefits transfer is important. Most benefits estimation methods involve some type of transfer. In fact, from a valuation standpoint benefits transfer is a natural extension of non-market valuation (Opaluch and Mazzotta, 1992). Unfortunately, the present state of non-market valuation does not adequately serve benefits transfer (Brookshire, 1992) because of the issues of aggregation and market scope. From a policy standpoint, information about benefits transfer is vital to non-market valuation in the current political and research climate (Feather and Hellerstein, 1997).

The valuation studies conducted in Pennsylvania, Georgia and Maine and reported in Chapters 2 and 4 of this book were designed both to estimate the value of protecting ground water from nitrate contamination and to facilitate development of a benefits transfer protocol. This chapter suggests, however, that even when using similar survey instruments across sites with nitrate contamination of ground water and similar socioeconomic characteristics, benefits are unlikely to be effectively transferred.

PREVIOUS STUDIES

The earliest acknowledged attempts at benefits estimates for environmental goods including non-market benefits were Eckstein's (1958) estimates and partial inclusion of what he called intangibles for water development projects. The next reference to benefits estimates came from the United States Forest Service's use of unit-day values for recreation demand estimates in 1962 (Loomis, 1992). Since then, benefits transfers have slowly gained acceptance in research and policy implementation, especially in the 1980's as researchers strove to extend the limited but growing number of benefits studies (Smith and Kaoru, 1990) and to develop new methods for valuing non-market goods. One of the driving forces behind the increasing number of benefits studies and better transfer estimates in the United States was Executive Order 12290, which mandated cost-benefit analysis for all major regulations (Kirchhoff *et al.*, 1997). Executive Order 12290 was, by many accounts, a political maneuver meant to reduce the burden on businesses by making it more difficult to enact environmental and other regulatory legislation. Ironically, the order led to a proliferation of focused, carefully constructed benefits studies which have supported the promulgation of regulations in the long run. The continued refinement of methods and the proliferation of benefits estimation studies has led to frequent use of benefits transfers in legal proceedings and government policy analyses where timely benefits estimates must rely on existing data (Boyle and Bergstrom, 1992).

Research on transfers peaked with the 1992 special issue of *Water Resources Research* in which the process and credibility of benefits transfers were discussed. Since then most work has relied on meta-analysis (van den Bergh and Button, 1997). While meta-analysis may be used for prediction, the primary advantage is that it forces researchers to document assumptions and judgements used in summarizing research results (Desvousges *et al.* 1998, p. 35).

The application of the meta-analysis approach to benefits transfer sometimes violates a primary tenet of scientific reasoning; the theoretical construct, or the object which the researcher attempts to measure, must be defined. That definition is less clear when several theoretical constructs are amalgamated. For example, when studies of several different ground water contaminants are combined in a meta-analysis, the results may be misleading. Concern about nitrates in ground water is probably different in significant ways from concern about carcinogenic chemical contaminants in ground water.

Another approach to benefits transfer is provided by Deck and Chestnut (1992). They provide a framework which examines the benefits transfer exercise from a marginal benefit/marginal cost perspective allowing both researcher and decision maker to determine beforehand precise criteria for the precision of transfers. The decision then depends upon the direction of possible error, the cost of a new study in the policy site versus the cost of potential error when using benefits transfer, and the decision maker's tolerance for uncertainty. More recently Desvousges *et al.* (1998) second this approach and have attempted to develop principles for consistent application of transfer methods.

Several practical studies have shown effective transfers for subjects other than ground water. While a number of studies have focused on benefits transfer of visibility (Smith and Osborne, 1996) and endangered species (Loomis and White, 1996), the bulk of the literature focuses on water issues. Most recently, Piper (1998) used the contingent valuation method to successfully validate a benefits transfer for a rural water system in Montana. Parsons and Kealy (1994) successfully modeled benefits transfers where transferred values deviated less than 10 percent from true values in their study of improving water quality for Milwaukee residents.

Other studies have identified difficulties or problems with benefits transfers approaches. Downing and Ozuna (1996) present evidence of benefits transfers overvaluing the benefits of recreational saltwater fishing. Alberini *et al.* (1997) compare three approaches to benefits transfer of WTP for avoiding health incidents and do not find relative improvements for functional transfers (using a complete demand function) indicating that a naive approach (using simple means) is just as good as a functional approach. Kirchhoff *et al.* (1997) use a tobit model in their investigation of recreation demand to conclude that estimates were imprecise even in cases where policy and study site had nearly identical characteristics.

Boyle and Bergstrom (1992) , and VandenBerg (1995) have outlined standards for benefits transfers for improvements in ground water safety. Boyle and Bergstrom (1992) especially stress the importance of examining bias in the original study. That is, if the original estimates at the study site are biased (the true mean at the study site is not equal to the estimated mean) then any transfer is fraught with potential error.

THEORY

The theory of benefits transfer is a direct extension of the theory of benefits measurement.   In effect, combining individual willingness to pay into aggregate demand functions for the good in question is a form of benefits transfer (Opaluch and Mazzotta, 1992). The transfer is from individual to sample via a function and from sample to population by simple scalar multiplication and adjustment for sample characteristics that do not match the population parameters. In this transfer study, benefits are transferred among samples from what is thought to be a single population.

Some previous work has erroneously relied on OLS to do functional transfers based on an assumption of normally distributed dependent variables. In concept, an individual's willingness to pay could be negative. But in practice, most individuals treat WTP as a zero censored variable, so the assumption of normality leads to biased and inefficient parameter estimates.

The model is designed to measure the consumer surplus of an improvement in ground water safety via a single program. As indicated in Chapter 1 of this book, the general treatment is to ask people about their WTP to receive a change from some baseline level Q^0 to some alternative level Q^1. While it is possible to bound their responses with a series of yes/no questions or a follow-up open-ended question, the initial focus is on analysis of the single-bounded approach. This means that the respondent's true WTP is bounded from below if they say 'yes' to the amount proposed and from above if the respondent says 'no'. With dichotomous-choice questions in either the single, double, or payment card versions however, the CV question provides only qualitative information about WTP. In order to obtain a quantitative estimate of WTP the researcher needs to link the yes/no answers to the payment amount in dollars that elicited their response (Hanemann and Kanninen 1996).

In a random utility context (referred to as Random Utility Maximization) the respondent seeks to maximize indirect utility V, a function of prices of market goods p, the proposed change Q, income I, socioeconomic characteristics H, and a random component ϵ: the bridge between what the researcher observes and those random components that the researcher cannot observe but which are completely understood by the respondent. Change in the indirect utility function is then written:

$$\Delta V = V(Q^1, p, I, H, \epsilon) - V(Q^0, p, I, H, \epsilon).$$

DATA

Data for the transfer exercise were taken from the three studies (for details see in this book Chapter 2 for Maine and Georgia and Chapter 4 for Pennsylvania). The questionnaires were administered in 1996 to measure the benefits of a program to protect ground water from nitrate contamination. The questionnaires were nearly identical in all three studies. Distributions of the bid amount in the dichotomous choice portion were derived from pretests conducted in Pennsylvania, Georgia, and Maine. The three studies were each divided into two portions with different question formats. The common format among all three studies was a dichotomous choice question asking for a yes/no response to a stated amount of a special tax to support a program designed to protect ground water from nitrate contamination. The dichotomous choice question was followed by an open-ended question asking the respondent to state the maximum amount his or her household would be willing to pay in a special tax to support the ground water protection program.

The Pennsylvania questionnaire also contained a group of questions testing respondents about what they knew about nitrate contamination of ground water — both about physical characteristics of ground water and about possible health effects. The test contained questions taken directly from the information section common to all three surveys. The inclusion of this information check made the Pennsylvania questionnaire somewhat longer than the Maine and Georgia surveys. Whether or not this extended version altered respondents' answers is unknowable.

The scenario description in the Pennsylvania questionnaire also differed from the others. It told respondents that adopting the proposed program would reduce the proportion of wells exceeding 10 ppm nitrate from the present 50% to 25%. The Georgia and Maine scenario descriptions did not indicate the target proportion of wells with nitrate contaminated water. In all three questionnaires, respondents were asked to indicate the present level of safety of their water supply as well as estimating the probability that their water would be safe ten years later, both with and without the proposed program.

The response rate for the Pennsylvania study was 68.4%. The response rates for the Georgia and the Maine studies were each 53%.

METHODS

The analysis follows a combination Kirchhoff *et al.* (1997) tobit approach, VandenBerg *et al.* general approach discussed in Chapter 6 of this book and Loomis (1992). VandenBerg *et al.* (Chapter 6, this book) used data from Powell's (one of the authors) dissertation which was tailor-made for benefits transfer of the benefits of protecting ground water from a variety of contaminants. Data was collected from nine sites grouped by contaminant using virtually the same survey instrument for each site. The approach used there is the model for our approach. We do not use OLS regression, however, since the OLS model does not take into account censoring, and thus may yield incorrect parameter estimates. We instead conduct the same functional transfers using probit and tobit models instead of the OLS model.

The results from the probit models are illustrative in showing how intrasite error (Boyle and Bergstrom, 1992) can be magnified through transfers. In other words, if we used the information contained in only the first part of the elicitation question (the yes/no part) variation in mean willingness to pay grows in magnitude when transferred. In the tobit models (examining responses to the follow-up open-ended question) the intrasite bias is reduced because of an experimentally induced bias — the bid amount acts as an anchor for valuation of a relatively unfamiliar good. The models used the same specification for all three sites for both probit and tobit models.

Evaluating the relative merits of these transfers is difficult because there are no established standards or benchmarks for acceptability. Since benefit estimates for environmental goods are scarce in public policy (relative to cost estimates) any available number is often deemed best. In this analysis, simple criteria are used to compare actual estimates with transfer estimates. In this study two approaches are employed. First, the naive approach compares means from both probit and tobit results. Second, there are six comparisons where the parameter estimates from each model are used to estimate benefits in each of the other two sites. In both approaches the test statistic is percentage error. For the probit models (the dichotomous-choice question) the percentage error is calculated for the prediction of 'yes' responses. That is, the actual number of 'yes' responses minus the predicted number of 'yes' responses divided by the actual number. We conclude by focusing on welfare estimates and the nature of the tradeoffs between using transfers and conducting an entirely new study.

The econometric approach was to find one model that theoretically suits *a priori* expectations of factors contributing to willingness to pay for ground water safety. An explicit decision was made to retain all theoretically relevant variables in our models. Although this may lead to the inclusion of statistically insignificant variables, it is preferable to excluding possibly relevant variables.

The independent variables are defined as follows: BID is the payment amount in the dichotomous choice portion of the question format. Perceived effectiveness of the program is the difference between the perceived level of safety with the program and the perceived level of safety without the program ($\Delta H_2OSAFETY$). Concern for water is a dummy variable equal to one if the respondent both places a high priority on local government expenditures for ground water protection and is concerned about ground water safety (CONCERN). I is a categorical income variable although it is treated as a continuous variable by using the midpoint values of each income category. PROACTIVE, another dummy variable, indicates that respondents have taken some type of averting action to avoid health risks due to ground water contamination in the past five years. PRIVATE WATER is a dichotomous variable representing the type of water supply as private well or public supply.

RESULTS

In the following analyses the data included all observations from the three sites except those which had missing values or a protest response to the valuation question. Protest bids were indicated by a respondent's answer to the question following the bid elicitation question. They indicate that the bid response included considerations other than the respondent's value of the ground water protection program. The protest bids were excluded to avoid confusion while estimating the value of the protection program. This procedure is appropriate for the purpose of this study — to estimate the value of protecting ground water and to determine the factors which influence respondents' bids. In this study the exclusion of protest responses did not alter the regional composition of the sample – for each site approximately 30% of the responses were protests.

Descriptive statistics for the independent variables for the combined sample and each site are found in Table 7.1. Means for the independent variables included in the analysis were strikingly similar across the three studies. The mean perception of the effectiveness of the program ($\Delta H_2OSAFETY$) was approximately equal in Maine and Pennsylvania, with a higher value in Georgia. Income (I) is statistically similar in Pennsylvania and Georgia, but significantly lower than these two in Maine. The three sites each have about 20% of the households with children under 13 years present (CHILDREN PRESENT). Roughly the same proportion of respondents in each area had a high concern for water safety, 60%. About the same proportion of respondents in Maine (43%) and Georgia (38%) had been proactive in undertaking averting measures to avoid possible harmful effects of ground water contamination. A substantially larger proportion of the Pennsylvania respondents had taken such action (63%). The areas also differ in the proportion of the respondents who obtain their water from private wells, with a little over two-thirds in Pennsylvania and Maine but only about one-quarter in Georgia having private wells.

Dichotomous Bids and WTP

Four models were run with the identical specification. Pennsylvania, Georgia, and Maine were run separately and a combined model was run (Table 7.2). The dependent variable is the yes/no response to one of eight payment amounts: $25, $50, $75, $100, $150, $200, $350 and $500. The independent variables are BID (the bid amount), $\Delta H_2OSAFETY$, CONCERN, I, PROACTIVE, CHILDREN PRESENT and PRIVATE WATER. In the combined model, all variables were significant at the 10 percent level or higher. The coefficient estimates for BID, $\Delta H_2OSAFETY$, CONCERN, and I were significant at better than the one percent level. The negative sign on BID was expected; as the program cost increases, the probability of a 'yes' response decreases. The signs on the other variables are as expected, except for CHILDREN PRESENT and PRIVATE WATER. The negative sign on CHILDREN PRESENT is counter to expectations since young children are most susceptible to adverse health effects. The sign on PRIVATE WATER is also counterintuitive — since the program benefits private well owners more than public water users, who are already protected by regulations.

Table 7.1. Descriptive statistics, PA, GA and ME benefits transfer study

	Combined Sample N=420		Pennsylvania N = 160		Georgia N= 121		Maine N=139	
	Mean	Std. Dev.	Mean	Std. Dev.	Mean	Std. Dev.	Mean	Std. Dev.
BID	174.76	150.36	168.59	147.76	179.13	157.86	178.06	147.46
$\Delta H_2OSAFETY$	15.57	25.51	13.96	27.56	21.12	26.63	12.59	21.12
CONCERN	0.58	0.49	0.58	0.49	0.64	0.48	0.54	0.50
I (thousands)	42.19	25.76	46.00	24.86	47.31	29.18	33.35	21.08
PROACTIVE	0.49	0.50	0.63	0.48	0.38	0.49	0.43	0.50
CHILDREN PRESENT	0.20	0.40	0.27	0.44	0.17	0.38	0.15	0.36
PRIVATE WATER	0.55	0.49	0.68	0.47	0.25	0.43	0.66	0.47

Table 7.2. *Marginal effects — probit results, PA, GA and ME benefits transfer study*

Variable	Combined	PA	GA	ME
Constant	-0.6566 [a] (0.1878)	-0.7985 [b] (0.3354)	0.0288 (0.3212)	-1.2788 [a] (0.3910)
BID	-0.0026 [a] (0.0005)	-0.0022 [a] (0.0008)	-0.0026 [a] (0.0008)	-0.0029 [a] (0.0009)
ΔH_2O-SAFETY	0.0204 [a] (0.0031)	0.0202 [a] (0.0051)	0.0196 [a] (0.0056)	0.0181 [a] (0.0066)
CONCERN	0.5248 [a] (0.1426)	0.5737 [b] (0.2392)	0.2362 (0.2662)	0.6740 [b] (0.2714)
I (thousands)	0.0068 [a] (0.0027)	0.0111 [b] (0.0047)	-0.0005 (0.0042)	0.0118 [c] (0.0065)
PRO-ACTIVE	0.2614 [c] (0.1421)	0.1768 (0.2461)	0.1467 (0.2616)	0.4186 [c] (0.2574)
CHILDREN PRESENT	-0.2788 [c] (0.1699)	-0.0881 (0.2539)	-0.3932 (0.3283)	-0.5506 (0.3720)
PRIVATE WATER	-0.2429 [c] (0.1407)	-0.3777 (0.2461)	-0.0523 (0.3006)	0.0733 (0.2817)
WTP (dollars)	65	70	205	-50
Percent 'yes'	42	42	53	31
Percent 'yes' predicted	37	38	61	24
Percentage error	12	10	15	23
Percentage correctly predicted	74	80	65	78

Notes
Standard errors in parentheses
[a]significant at the 1 percent level
[b]significant at the 5 percent level
[c]significant at the 10 percent level

In the Pennsylvania model, PROACTIVE, CHILDREN PRESENT and PRIVATE WATER are insignificant, while in Georgia only BID and $\Delta H_2OSAFETY$ remain significant. In Maine all variables are significant except CHILDREN PRESENT and PRIVATE WATER.

There are two issues that we address while transferring benefits. The first is whether models representing different sites reflect the same underlying preferences. The second issue is how well models represent their respective populations. We tested whether the models are generated from the same underlying utility function (the combined model) using likelihood ratio tests. In each case the null hypothesis that the models derive from the same underlying parameter vector can be rejected at the 95% level.

The combined model correctly predicts 74% of the outcomes. The Pennsylvania model predicts 80% correctly, while the Georgia model predicts approximately two-thirds correctly and the Maine model predicts correctly nearly 80% of the responses. Because the percent of 'yes' responses differs greatly across the sites (Table 7.2), we calculated an error percentage to measure the effectiveness of the model at each site. We subtracted the percent of predicted 'yes' answers from the actual percentage of 'yes' answers in the sample from each site and divided that difference by the actual value. This provides a relative measure of the estimation error. The Pennsylvania sample had 42% 'yes' responses and the model predicted there would be 38% 'yes' answers. The evaluation yielded a 10% error. The Georgia sample, however, had 53% 'yes' answers and the model predicted 61%, yielding a 15% error. For the Maine sample there were 31% 'yes' answers and the model predicted 24% yielding a 23% error.

Open-Ended Bids and WTP

In designing the study, we included the open-ended follow-up question to provide a second bound on the bid elicitation effort. The dichotomous choice question provided the first bound. The change in the type of question was intentional; the respondent first encountered a question requiring a qualitative response (yes/no) and then a question that required a quantitative refinement of the initial response. One might argue that the results from the open-ended follow-up question are experimentally induced or at least conditioned by the distribution of bid amounts used in the prior dichotomous choice question. Therefore it is no surprise that the open-ended values were highly correlated with the bid amounts in the dichotomous choice question. In this setting they are, in fact, the result of revisions of the respondents' initial answers.

In order to evaluate the open-ended question we used a tobit model (see Table 7.3). The overall mean willingness to pay of the combined sample is $80.29, whereas Pennsylvania's mean is $82.90, Georgia's mean is $104.71, and Maine's is $60.56. A simple comparison of means and confidence intervals of the dependent variable, willingness to pay, shows that the samples yielded very different results.

The tobit regressions show that coefficients on the regressors are comparable. Table 7.3 presents the marginal effects; the coefficients are the partial derivatives of expected value with respect to the vector of characteristics, calculated at the means of the X's. All independent variables retain significant coefficients in the combined model. In the Pennsylvania model all coefficients are significant except CONCERN and CHILDREN PRESENT. The Georgia model has significant coefficients on BID, $\Delta H_2OSAFETY$, CHILDREN PRESENT and PRIVATE WATER. In the Maine model the CONSTANT, BID, $\Delta H_2OSAFETY$ and CONCERN are significant. The coefficient values themselves are indicative of the marginal effects of the independent variables on WTP (adjusted by the scale factor).

The overall model with 403 observations (after removing protest responses) is used to calculate the predicted values of the individual sites. The predicted values in the next to the last row of Table 7.3 show a means of $92.71 for Pennsylvania compared to the conditional mean (third row from the bottom of Table 7.3) of $82.90 which happens to be the same as the sample mean – $82.90. For Georgia the predicted mean is $109.14 compared to the sample mean of $99.13 and a conditional mean of $104.71. For Maine the predicted mean value is $78.03 relative to a sample mean of $60.94 and a conditional mean of $60.56.

We also calculated an error percentage to evaluate the effectiveness of the model at each site. For this calculation we subtracted the predicted mean from the conditional mean and divided by the predicted mean to obtain an estimated error. For all three sites the predicted mean is larger than the conditional mean so the percentage error is a negative number. The Pennsylvania sample had -10.5% error while the Georgia error was -4.2% and the error for the Maine sample was -22.4%.

The probit and tobit estimates of mean WTP for the combined sample and each of the sites are presented in Table 7.4. The last row of the table shows the difference in the two estimates for each sample. The estimated WTP is about the same for the combined sample and Pennsylvania, but there are substantial differences between the two estimates for Georgia and Maine.

Transfers

Since the results of the tobit analysis are thought to be affected by the respondents anchoring on the values presented to them in the dichotomous-choice question, the remainder of our analysis uses the results of the probit regressions. If one were to perform a naive benefits transfer using the value of the mean WTP at one site as the estimate of the mean WTP at another site, there will be substantial errors of estimation in almost every case. For example, if the probit estimate for the Pennsylvania site ($70) were used to estimate the mean WTP of either the Georgia or Maine sites, it would underestimate the Georgia value by $135 and overestimate the Maine value by

Table 7.3. Marginal effects — tobit models without protests, PA, GA and ME benefits transfer study

	Combined	PA	GA	ME
Variable N=	403	155	115	133
Constant	-63.1960[a]	-73.7730[a]	-45.6610	-62.2820[a]
	(11.3860)	(19.8960)	(25.1590)	(16.1510)
BID	0.2295[a]	0.2897[a]	0.2386[a]	0.1596[a]
	(0.0289)	(0.0492)	(0.0641)	(0.0396)
ΔH_2O-SAFETY	1.6062[a]	1.6956[a]	2.0587[a]	0.9956[a]
	(0.1949)	(0.2813)	(0.4413)	(0.3268)
CONCERN	18.4920[b]	12.4770	-6.1691	26.8650[a]
	(8.9377)	(14.7230)	(21.0260)	(12.1720)
I (thousands)	0.5519[a]	0.61855[b]	0.3147	0.7280[a]
	(0.1688)	(0.2830)	(0.3309)	(0.2777)
PROACTIVE	22.9670[b]	42.4720[b]	8.4867	9.6185
	(8.7270)	(14.8590)	(19.7630)	(11.5460)
CHILDREN PRESENT	25.1350[c]	15.1440	40.4370[c]	34.5900[c]
	(14.6670)	(22.3600)	(22.8930)	(20.8610)
PRIVATE WATER	-14.5190[c]	-27.664[b]	-30.8430	6.6561
	(8.6733)	(12.9520)	(22.6410)	(12.2410)
pseudo R-squared	0.237	0.254	0.134	0.233
WTP (dollars)	80.29	82.90	104.71	60.56
PREDICTED	na	92.71	109.14	78.03
PERCENTAGE ERROR	na	-10.51	-4.23	-22.38

Notes
Standard errors in parentheses
[a]significant at the 1 percent level
[b]significant at the 5 percent level
[c]significant at the 10 percent level

Table 7.4. *Directly estimated WTP (dollars), PA, GA and ME benefits transfer study*

	Combined	Pennsylvania	Georgia	Maine
Probit	65	70	205	-50
Tobit	80	83	105	61
Difference	-15	-13	100	-111

Table 7.5. *Probit WTP estimates using functional transfers (dollars), PA, GA and ME benefits transfer study*

	Pennsylvania Parameters	Georgia Parameters	Maine Parameters
Pennsylvania Data	70	139	25
Georgia Data	212	205	60
Maine Data	-23	135	-50

$120. If one chose to use the tobit estimates of the mean values the errors are smaller, but still larger than most policy analysts are willing to accept.

If one chose to use a functional transfer instead of the naive transfer, the results are not encouraging either. In Table 7.5 the columns show the results of using the parameter estimates of the model for the indicated site with the data from the site indicated by the row heading. Thus, the three estimates of the mean WTP for the Pennsylvania site are shown in the top row: $70 using the Pennsylvania model, $139 using the Georgia model and $25 using the Maine model. Similarly the three estimates for the Georgia site are in the second row and for the Maine site in the third row. In a few cases the estimates are reasonably close together, e.g., Georgia data using Pennsylvania or Georgia parameters, but there remain cases which exhibit large errors.

IMPLICATIONS AND CONCLUSIONS

Many researchers express an aversion to benefits transfer. They consider estimates of benefits that are transferred from other studies as imperfect measures subject to uncertain variation depending on the context. Even when transfers are expressed in ranges instead of as point estimates they are considered to be dangerously fleeting and may be illusory. Benefits estimates are highly susceptible to biases in the data generating process and these biases can be exacerbated by biases in the transfer processes.

Yet, policy makers need estimates of benefits, even if they are imperfect. The cost of not providing timely estimates may be high both in terms of the widening chasm between theory and application and by depriving policy decision-makers of information from cost-benefit analysis. The costs of not having benefits information when making a decision must be weighed against the costs of possibly inaccurate or misleading benefits transfer work, for a wrong decision made with defective information also imposes costs. The ultimate test is whether the expected cost of doing the transfer, including the costs of making the wrong decision, outweighs the cost of doing a complete benefits study (which also is susceptible to error).

In this chapter we provide evidence of cases where a new study may be necessary and cases where transfers may suffice. Difference in mean and median WTP was significant and highly variable with dichotomous choice models but closed rapidly with the addition of a follow-up open-ended question. In short, estimates are easily manipulated and sensitive to methodological changes. Similarly, using the benefits value at one site as the predicted benefits of another would give poor results for benefits transfer in most instances studied.

Past benefits transfer studies have relied on an *ad hoc* approach to questionnaire design and the use of meta-analysis. Meta-analysis is a quick and relatively cost-effective way of supplementing and highlighting information about benefits estimates (van den Bergh and Button, 1997), but not a satisfactory transfer tool. Therefore, it is not astonishing that their results have concluded that benefits transfers may be impossible. This impossibility hypothesis (called a myth by Boyle and Bergstrom, 1992) is reinforced in this chapter, where it is shown that careful study design and consistency of instrument choice may not mitigate the factors that had previously led to similarly unsatisfactory results for transferring benefits.

The reasons for the relative accuracy of the transfer using studies that employ the open-ended follow-up are most likely artifacts of the experiment. The primary reason is anchoring. Anchoring may be more severe due to the nature of the good and therefore the effectiveness of transfers depends on the nature of the good. Ground water is not seen and is difficult to monitor. Respondents may have been sufficiently conditioned by the bid payment values to ensure that effective transfers were figments of our imaginative questionnaire construction, analogous to leading a witness in a courtroom. On the other hand, since water is bought and sold, experience with paying for water is commonplace. Therefore, asking respondents about ground water improvement via higher payments has an aspect of market realism that is not found with many other environmental goods.

REFERENCES

Alberini, Anna, Maureen Cropper, Tsu-Tan Fu, Alan Krupnick, Jin-Tan Liu, Daigee Shaw and Winston Harrington (1997), 'Valuing health effects of air pollution in developing countries: the case of Taiwan,' *Journal of Environmental Economics and Management*, **34**:107-26.

Bingham, Tayler H., (ed.) (1992), *Benefits Transfer: Procedures, Problems, and Research Needs,* Proceedings of the Association of Environmental and Resource Economists Workshop, Snowbird, Utah, June 3-5.

Boyle, Kevin and John Bergstrom (1992), 'Benefit transfer studies: myths, pragmatism, and idealism,' *Water Resources Research*, **28**:657-63.

Brookshire, David S. (1992), 'Issues regarding benefits transfer,' from *Benefits Transfer: Procedures, Problems, and Research Needs* proceedings of the Association of Environmental and Resource Economists Workshop, Snowbird Utah, June 3-5.

Deck, Leland B. and Lauraine G. Chestnut (1992), 'How good is good enough?,' From *Benefits Transfer: Procedures, Problems, and Research Needs,* Proceedings of the Association of Environmental and Resource Economists Workshop, Snowbird Utah, June 3-5.

Desvousges, William H., Michael C. Naughton and George R. Parsons (1992), 'Benefit transfer: conceptual problems in estimating water quality benefits using existing studies,' *Water Resources Research*, **28**:675-83.

Desvousges, William H.., F. Reed Johnson and H. Spencer Banzhaf (1998), *Environmental Policy Analysis with Limited Information: Principles and Applications of the Transfer Method,* Edward Elgar: Cheltenham, UK and Lyme, US.

Downing and Ozuna (1996), 'Testing the reliability of the benefit function transfer approach,' *Journal of Environmental Economics and Management*, **30**:316-22.

Eckstein, Otto (1958), *Water Resource Development,* Harvard University Press: Cambridge, Massachusetts.

Feather, Peter and Daniel Hellerstein (1997), 'Calibrating benefit function transfer to assess the conservation reserve program,' *American Journal of Agricultural Economics*, **79**:151-62.

Hanemann, Michael and Barbara Kanninen (1996), 'The statistical analysis of discrete response CV data,' Department of Agricultural and Resource Economics, University of California at Berkeley, California Experiment Station, Giannini Foundation of Agricultural Economics, June.

Kask, Susan F. and Jason F. Shogren (1994), 'Benefit transfer protocol for long-term health risk valuation: a case of surface water contamination,' *Water Resources Research*, **30**:2813-23.

Kirchhoff, Stefanie, Bonnie G. Colby and Jeffrey T. LaFrance (1997), 'Evaluating the performance of benefit transfer: an empirical inquiry,' *Journal of Environmental Economics and Management*, **33**:75-93.

Loomis, John B. (1992), 'The evolution of a more rigorous approach to benefit transfer: benefit function transfer,' *Water Resources Research*, **28**: 701-705.

Loomis, John B. and Douglas White (1996), 'Economic benefits of rare and endangered species: summary and meta-analysis,' *Ecological Economics*, **18**:197-206.

Opaluch, James and Marisa J. Mazzotta (1992), 'Fundamental issues in benefit transfer and natural resource damage assessment,' from *Benefits Transfer: Procedures, Problems, and Research Needs,* Proceedings of the Association of Environmental and Resource Economists Workshop. Snowbird Utah, June 3-5.

Parsons, George R. and Mary Jo Kealy (1994), 'Benefits transfer in a random utility model of recreation,' *Water Resources Research*, **30**:2477-84.

Piper, Steven (1998), 'Using contingent valuation and benefit transfer to evaluate water supply improvement benefits,' *Journal of the American Water Resources Association*, **34**:311-20.

Smith, V. Kerry and Yoshiaki Kaoru (1990), 'Signals or noise? Explaining the variation in recreation benefit estimates,' *American Journal of Agricultural Economics*, **72**:419-33.

Smith, V. Kerry and Laura Osborne (1996), 'Do contingent valuation estimates pass a scope test? A meta-analysis,' *Journal of Environmental Economics and Management*, **31**:287-301.

VandenBerg, T.P. (1995), 'Assessing the accuracy of benefits transfers: evidence from a multi-site contingent valuation study of groundwater quality,' unpublished masters thesis, Cornell University, Ithaca, NY.

van den Bergh, C. J. M. Jeroen, and Kenneth J. Button (1997), 'Meta-analysis of environmental issues in regional, urban and transport economics,' *Urban Studies*, **34**:927-44.

8. A Preliminary Meta Analysis of Contingent Values for Ground Water Quality Revisited

Gregory L. Poe, Kevin J. Boyle, and John C. Bergstrom

INTRODUCTION

In 1994, we collaborated on an Association of Environmental and Resource Economics/American Association of Agricultural Economics invited paper entitled 'What do we know about groundwater values? Preliminary implications from a meta analysis of contingent-valuation studies' (Boyle *et al.* 1994). At that time, application of contingent valuation methods to ground water quality was still very novel, beginning with Edwards' pioneering paper in 1988. And thus the number of data points in our study were limited to a selection of unique estimates that could be gleaned from the eight studies that had been completed through early 1994. Given this small base, we cautiously adopted a meta-analysis approach using estimated values from individual studies 'to statistically investigate whether the eight contingent valuation studies of ground water protection collectively provide a richer picture of the benefits from ground water protection than can be developed from a qualitative comparison of the study features and results' (p. 1055). In pursuing this effort our intent was not to identify absolute magnitudes of coefficients or an equation that would serve as a base for benefit transfers of estimated ground water values to unstudied sites. We acknowledged that such a pursuit would be misleading and premature. Rather, we simply sought to explore whether there was a systematic consistency across studies. We were pleasantly surprised: concluding that 'ground water valuation studies, despite their limitations, are not producing random noise. These studies are reflecting systematic differences in ground water values...' (p. 1060).

The present study builds upon our original work in 1994. It differs however in a number of dimensions. First, our library of studies to draw from has broadened with the addition of new studies conducted by Crutchfield *et al.* (1997), Delavan (1997), and Bergstrom *et al.* in Chapter 2 (this book), and revisiting of data that was still nascent in 1994 (e.g., Bergstrom and Dorfman, 1994; Poe, 1998). This additional data has allowed us to reevaluate our selection of observations for the application and to modify the composition of explanatory variables. Our empirical analysis differs from the previous work in that instead of treating each unique value as an equally weighted observation, each study is now given equal weight. That is, a study with 23 observations has equal weight in this analysis as a study that provides two observations. Adopting an equal weighting approach across studies dilutes the effects of additional within-study observations – which was of substantial concern in our 1994 data – and allows us to be less parsimonious in our selection of data points. Willingness-to-pay values have been updated to 1997 dollars and we now use a linear, as opposed to a log-linear, function in our analyses.

This chapter is organized as follows. Building on the ideas expressed in Chapter 1 and subsequent chapters of this book, the next section provides a broad conceptual framework for our analyses. With an eye towards the meta analysis we then briefly review the individual studies and identify the variables to be used. The results and implications from this research are discussed in the final two sections.

CONCEPTUAL FRAMEWORK

Following Glass's (1976) article describing the meta-analysis approach, this term refers to 'the statistical analysis of a large collection of results for individual studies for the purposes of integrating the findings. It connotes a rigorous alternative to the casual, narrative discussion of research studies which typify our attempt to make some sense of the rapidly expanding research literature' (p. 3). As noted by van den Bergh *et al.* (1997) this technique has a major potential for developing a consensus on point estimates in the valuation of environmental goods and for exploring factors that have influenced variations within and across individual studies:

> Meta-Approaches may be used to summarize over a collection of similar relationships and indicators, or to average, possibly using weights, over a collection of values obtained in similar studies. It is suited to this because point estimates are, by definition, quantified and, hence, conventional statistical methods can usually be applied with relative ease' (p. 5).

Correspondingly several studies have used this technique to synthesize valuation research concerning a range of environmental goods, including urban pollution valuation, visibility improvement, recreation benefits, and noise nuisance (see van den Bergh *et al.*, 1997).

The present meta analysis builds upon the conceptual framework in Chapter 1 (this book), which implicitly defines willingness to pay as a state independent option price (OP) in a utility difference framework. This framework provides the basic insight for identifying the variables that need to be included in the meta analysis to control for differences in structure and approach in the various contingent valuation studies. Option price is derived from a change in ground water quality and related economic factors entering the indirect utility function. As such, the change in the probability that a water supply is contaminated, the price of water and its substitutes, and income level, should be considered core economic variables.

In moving from the conceptual framework to field application, it is clear that other methodological effects need to be accounted for if we are to try to isolate the critical economic features affecting option price. As noted frequently in the contingent valuation literature, reported values are context dependent. As a result, the type of information provided to participants and other programmatic features particular to the described ground water protection program should be incorporated into the meta analysis. Accumulated laboratory experiments and field research also suggest that values provided are not invariant to the elicitation method. And thus, the elicitation method needs to be accounted for in the empirical analysis. Each of these issues, which we shall group under core economic variables and study design effects will be discussed in detail in the 'Meta Analysis Variables' section. We now turn to characterizing the studies that serve as a base for this analysis.

STUDY DESCRIPTIONS

The existing set of ground water studies represents a continuum of ideas and methods, from which there are numerous ways one might try to categorize them into a sensible framework. From an organizational perspective we group the 13 studies considered in this analysis into three categories. The first category follows Edwards' (1988) focus on evaluating specific changes in water quality. The second category focuses on studies that evaluated water quality changes presented in more general terms. The third category instead frames the valuation problem as affecting the quantity, as opposed to the quality of water, available to the community. These three groups are termed specific quality change, general quality change, and quantity change models, respectively. In creating this taxonomy, we clearly recognize that there are a number of alternative ways that the data might be partitioned. The studies included in each category are discussed below. Boyle (1994) provides additional discussion of the studies contained in our 1994 paper. Numbers in [ ] refer to the year the survey was conducted.

It is important to note that the entirety of published ground water studies are not included in the present analysis. Several worthy studies simply did not have enough cohorts along a critical methodological dimension and, hence, were precluded from this meta analysis. Omitted studies include research that was conducted outside the United States (e.g., Hanley, 1989; Stenger and Willinger, 1998), that reported values for marginal or incremental changes in contamination (e.g, Sparco, 1995; Poe and Bishop, 1999), or that used alternative value elicitation techniques such as conjoint analysis (e.g., Stevens *et al.*, 1997). The Randall *et al.* study reported in Chapter 5 of this book was also omitted because of its broader focus on valuing wetlands and surface and ground water and its use of a one-time as opposed to an annual payment.

Specific Quality Change Studies

The common theme in these studies is that specific information is provided, for example in a survey questionnaire, that allows respondents to assign particular target and reference (e.g., 'with' and 'without') water quality levels to their own household's water supply. For example, a participant might be asked to assume that, without a program, their own household would face a 75 percent probability of exceeding government health standards for a given contaminant (i.e., $PROB^0 = 0.75$). They are then asked to value a program that would reduce that probability to, say, zero (i.e., $PROB^1 = 0$). Thus, in this example, as in Edwards' (1988) study, the program guarantees that the pollution levels in a respondent's well will not exceed government health standards. As an alternative to specifying 'objective' probabilities for the participant, 'subjective' approaches allow individuals to identify subjective probabilities of contamination. We now briefly describe each of the studies in this category.

Edwards [1986]: Edwards introduced the probability of contamination threshold approach in a study that considered the issue of nitrate contamination in the Falmouth and Woods Hole communities in Cape Cod. Using a mail survey, participants were asked to 'assume that there is a ___ percent chance that all ground water in Falmouth and Cape Cod will be contaminated with nitrate from sewage 5 years from now if nothing new is done to protect it', wherein the reference probability of contamination varied across a split-sample design and included 25%, 50%, 75% and 100%. The target condition with the program was either that 'nitrate contamination will definitely be prevented' or that 'the chances of contamination are reduced to 25%'.[1]   A dichotomous choice response format was used to elicit values, and analyzed in a utility-theoretic framework that isolated option price as a measure of mean willingness to pay. Values for the meta analysis are taken from measures associated with

25%, 50%, 75% and 100% reductions in probabilities of contamination presented in Table III in Edwards (1988).

Sun [1989]: As reported in Sun (1990), Sun *et al.* (1992), and Bergstrom and Dorfman (1994), this study adapted Edwards' (1988) approach to include subjective perceptions of the reference probability of contamination. In a mail survey, respondents were asked, 'If nothing new is done to prevent ground water pollution in your area do you expect your sources of drinking and cooking water to become polluted by agricultural pesticides and fertilizers during the next five years?', with response options ranging from 'Yes, Definitely (100 percent certain)' to 'No, Definitely Not (0 percent chance)' in 25% increments. The target condition was that pollution of ground water will definitely be kept at safe levels (that is, *below* the United States health advisory levels of 10 mg/l NO_3-N). The methodological focus of this research was to assess the effects of information on contingent values for ground water. Using a split sample design, approximately an equal number of respondents received one of the following variants: 1) no additional information about the contamination levels; 2) information discussing the sources, types, and levels of contamination associated with agricultural fertilizers and pesticides; 3) information discussing the possible health effects associated with contamination from agricultural pesticides and fertilizers; or 4) both types of information described in 2) and 3). Values were elicited using a dichotomous choice question, followed by an open-ended question. Those values used in the meta analysis include follow-up open-ended values associated with each information level (Sun, 1990), three mean dichotomous choice values estimated from a pooled information data set using an *ad hoc* option price framework for 0%, 54% and 100% without-program subjective probabilities of contamination (Sun *et al.*, 1992), and 12 observations from differing reference probabilities of contamination (25%, 50%, 75%, and 100%) and information group combinations estimated using a utility-theoretic analytical framework (Bergstrom and Dorfman, 1994).

Jordan and Elnagheeb [1991]: Jordan and Elnagheeb (1993) elicited values for a ground water treatment/filtration program in Georgia using a mail survey. Current water quality conditions were not specified, but respondents were asked to assume that nitrate levels in water exceeded safety standards (for private well owners) or were increasing (for public well owners). Using a payment card elicitation framework, private well owners were then asked how much they would pay for installing and maintaining new treatment equipment on their well 'to avoid the risk of increasing nitrates in my drinking water'. Those attached to public supplies were asked how much they would be willing to pay in increased costs on their monthly water bill for treating water with increasing levels of nitrate contamination. The methodological focus was on comparisons of ordinary least squares and maximum likelihood methods of modeling payment card responses, as well as differences in mean willingness to pay associated with private and public well users. Mean and median willingness-to-pay values were taken from Jordan and Elnagheeb's preferred maximum likelihood estimates (without protest bids) for public and private well users.

Poe [1991-92]: The Poe study closely corresponds with the Sun (1990) research. As discussed by Poe and Bishop in Chapter 3 of this book, the reference contamination conditions were subjectively specified by the respondents using a scale similar to that used by Sun, target conditions were to reduce the probability of exceeding health standards to zero, an *ad hoc* dichotomous choice framework was used to estimate willingness-to-pay distributions, and information was varied across samples. The methodological focus of this mail survey of rural residents with private wells was the effect of information on risk perceptions (Poe *et al.* 1998) and willingness to pay (Poe and Bishop, Chapter 3, this book). The study consisted of two sequential stages. Respondents to the first stage (listed in Tables 8.1 and 8.2 as Poe Stage I) were asked to base their values on their existing knowledge of their household water quality, with approximately one half receiving no additional information and the other half receiving general information about the sources of nitrates, the health effects of nitrates, government standards for nitrates , and possible averting options. Separate no-information and with-information mean willingness-to-pay values for this first stage of the study are taken from Poe and Bishop (1992). In the second stage (listed in Tables 8.1 and 8.2 as Poe Stage II), respondents were provided with general information of the type described above along with specific information about their water quality based on an actual nitrate test of their household water supply. For the meta analysis 10 observations associated with 0%, 25% , 50%, 75%, and 100% change in probability of exceeding government standards were taken from the Stage II survey. Five of these 10 were median willingness-to-pay values taken from Poe (1998) and the other five were mean values reported in Chapter 3 of this book. In classifying the two stages as separate studies in this analysis, we maintain that the information conditions were different enough so as to constitute separate samples.

Crutchfield [1994]: This study deviated from the other research used in the meta analysis in that it was included in a national telephone survey conducted as part of the National Survey of Recreation and the Environment. Questions regarding drinking water appeared in the middle of the survey, following a set of questions on water-based recreation activities. The reference and target conditions for both private and public well users was 'Suppose your home tap water is contaminated by nitrates to a level that exceeds the EPA's minimum standard by 50%. However, assume that the local agency could install and maintain a filter in your home to the minimum safety standards set by the EPA... Note that if you chose not to have this filter installed, nitrate will be present in your tap water at the original levels.' A second question was asked that indicated that 'due to technological advances, instead of only partially eliminating nitrates, this system can completely eliminate nitrates from your tap water', begging the question of whether the EPA safety standard is regarded by respondents as safe. The authors found a premium for the more effective filter came to about 3 percent over the standard filter, suggesting some nominal additional value for moving beyond the threshold. The study was conducted in four regions of the US -- the Mid-Columbia basin in Washington State, Central Nebraska, White River Basin in Illinois, and the Lower Susquehanna River in Pennsylvania. Altogether, this study provided eight mean willingness-to-pay values for the meta analysis derived from dichotomous choice question formats. These values were incorporated into the specific quality change category by assuming that the change in probability equaled 100% for both types of filter.

General Quality Change Studies

Whereas the specific information studies provide information on specific water quality levels for a household's own water supply, general quality change studies provide information that only generally describes water quality levels, say from a regional or an average perspective. That is, emphasis is given to describing and valuing a comprehensive program, without specifying changes in outcomes for a household's own water supply. For example, in a survey questionnaire people may be told that currently 50% of private wells in a region are contaminated, and that a protection program will reduce this probability to 25%. With only this information to work from, an individual would not know specific water quality levels with and without a protection program for his or her own household's water supply.

Shultz [1988]: As described in Shultz (1989) and Schultz and Lindsay (1990), this study used a mail survey to elicit willingness to pay for a ground water protection program in Dover, New Hampshire. Reference conditions were established by informing respondents that 'several other nearby N.H. towns have recently had their ground water supplies contaminated... On the other hand, many N.H. towns have never had any serious ground water pollution problems.' An alternative program was then described as an 'attempt' to protect community water supplies by 'purchasing land overlying sensitive ground water areas, formulating stricter zoning ordinances, hiring inspectors to enforce ground water pollution laws and standards and a variety of other strategies.' After specifying that these protection plans cannot guarantee the prevention of ground water pollution, but are instead intended to reduce the risk of such problems occurring, a dichotomous choice willingness-to-pay response was asked for the program. The meta analysis uses the mean and median willingness-to-pay values reported in Shultz and Lindsay (1990).

Powell [1989]: This mail survey was conducted in 12 towns across three northeastern states (see Chapter 6 in this book). The survey was conducted as part of a study of how the information gained from contingent valuation research could be used in ground water managers in local communities (see Powell, 1991 and Powell *et al.*, 1994). After noting that 'Many areas in the northeastern United States are discovering actual or potential threats to drinking water supplies,' individuals were asked to identify those sources that they feel are likely to contaminate their local ground water supplies in the future. Using pen and ink drawings as an aid, options included agricultural chemicals (pesticides, fertilizer), landfills, toxic chemicals (use, storage, disposal), accidental spills (road, rail, pipeline), underground storage tanks, and septic tanks. Subjects then identified the safety level of their current household supply, with safety response options including 'very safe,' 'safe,' 'somewhat safe,' and 'unsafe,' each with an associated descriptive paragraph for clarification. An 'area wide special water protection district' was described, and a payment card method was used to elicit willingness-to-pay values for a program that would move their water quality from their specified safety level to a 'very safe' level. Willingness-to-pay values and other data for the 12 towns were taken from VandenBerg *et al.* (Chapter 6, this book), Powell (1991), and access to the original data.

Caudill [1990]:   This study used a mail survey to obtain statewide estimates for prevention and well protection programs in Michigan. Respondents were asked to specify their risk of 'death from ground water pollution' in Michigan using 22 comparative risks ranging from chicken pox (0.1 deaths per million) to heart disease (3,306 deaths per million) on a reference risk ladder. The prevention scenario used an open-ended format to elicit willingness to pay for a program that 'would prevent any further increase in ground water pollution in your county' by identifying sources of ground water pollution and taking 'educational, regulatory and legal action'. An alternative well protection scenario would eliminate the 'remaining health threat from ground water pollution' by testing all wells for harmful chemicals once a year, and installing and maintaining filtration devices for water used by a household to remove any harmful chemicals that are detected. A complete program included both the prevention and well treatment activities. Six values are taken from Caudill's (1992) dissertation: rural and urban values for prevention, well protection, and the complete program.

Delavan [1996]:   In the Delavan (1997) study, the reference conditions for a ground water protection program specified that 'Currently, only about 50% of all private wells in your area have nitrate levels which meet the safety standard of 10 milligrams per liter. In some places the nitrates per liter are well above the standard while in other places the water is "safe" to drink'. The target conditions were described as a program that 'would improve the quality of water so that in 10 years 75% of the private wells will meet the standard'. The mail survey was conducted in Lancaster and Lebannon countries in southwestern Pennsylvania. As described in Chapter 4 of this book, the dichotomous choice questions were followed up with an open-ended question. Five values from Delavan's (1997) research were used in the meta analysis, two protest/no protest informed-open-ended, two protest/no protest open-ended-after-dichotomous-choice values, and the dichotomous choice value reported for Pennsylvania by Epp and Delavan in Chapter 4 of this book.

Bergstrom [1997] and *Boyle [1997]*: As reported in the Chapter 2 of this book, parallel valuation studies of ground water protection programs were conducted in Dougherty County, Georgia (Bergstrom) and Aroostook County, Maine (Boyle) using a questionnaire similar in most respects to that used by Delavan (1997). The studies were conducted in 1997 and are referred to in Tables 8.1 and 8.2 as Bergstrom [1997] and Boyle [1997]. Monitoring data was referred to in order to establish reference conditions indicating that 98% of public and private wells in Dougherty County have nitrate levels that meet safety standards (87% in the Maine study), suggesting that ground water in most places in the county is 'safe' to drink. The target conditions described a technical and financial ground water program that would protect and maintain this 'safe' level of ground water quality. Values were elicited using a dichotomous choice question. Building on the safety difference approach introduced in Powell (1991), safety values with and without the program were elicited using a 0 (definitely will not remain safe) to 100 (definitely will remain safe) scale.[2] Nine willingness-to-pay values were drawn from each of these studies. *Ad hoc* WTP values estimated using the Hanemann (1984) and Cameron (1988) approaches were taken from the protest and no-protest estimations presented under Model 1 in Table 2.2a and Table 2.2b in this book. Hanemann (1984) and Cameron (1988) WTP values based on the utility theoretic model reported in Table 2.3 in this book were also included. Finally, the 9th observation for each study was the open-ended value as reported in Table 7.3 in this book.

The Bergstrom *et al.* study conducted in Maine and Georgia and the Delavan (1997) study conducted in Pennsylvania (Chapters 2 and 4 of this book) were conducted as part of a benefits transfer exercise (Chapter 7, this book). Each of these three efforts provides a rich information set about nitrates (containing information boxes about 'How does ground water exist underground?, 'Nitrates in Ground water,' 'Potential health effects of nitrates: blue baby syndrome,' and 'Potential health effects of nitrates: cancer') and monitoring data was referred to in order to establish reference conditions for each region.

Quantity Change Studies (ΔSUPPLY)

McClelland et al. [1991]: The conceptual framework presented here and in Chapter 1 (this book) focuses on a change in quality or risk of exposure. This poses a problem when valuing public water supplies, because the quality of such supplies are already protected by the Safe Drinking Water Act (SDWA) standards. Such a contradiction seems to have been noticed by most studies that have included participants attached to public water supplies. For example,

Edwards (1988) included a direction indicating that 'Health risks are not listed because water quality is being monitored to protect us from using contaminated water.' Similarly, the Crutchfield *et al.* (1997) and Jordan and Elnagheeb (1993) studies include separate valuation scenarios for respondents using private supplies and respondents attached to municipal or public supplies.

McClelland *et al* [1991] as reported in McClelland *et al.* (1992), directly addressed the public supply issue by characterizing the situation as a supply shortage problem in a national mail survey. That is, reflecting real policy situations, public or community water that is contaminated has to either be treated to meet SDWA safety standards, or not used. In the latter case, a rationing program may be necessary. Water that is threatened can also be contained or otherwise isolated.

In the McClelland *et al.* (1992) report to the USEPA, various strategies to protect drinking water were evaluated using a split-sample design and a payment card elicitation technique. In all versions the contamination was described as a slow-moving plume emanating from a landfill. All participants were asked to value a complete clean-up program that would pump and clean up the contaminated water. A containment option that would stop the spread of the plume and draw household water from outside the containment area was offered to a sub-sample of respondents. Willingness to pay for a public treatment program was elicited from another sub-sample. Yet a third sub-sample was asked to consider rationing where water rationing would require cuts in water use of 10% and 70%. Finally, separate use values were derived from the complete clean-up approach with a sequence of embedding questions in which individuals were asked to identify the proportion of their stated values that were directed to environmental good causes in general and the proportion of values that specifically addressed their personal benefits from this ground water protection program. Using this technique, which is described in detail in Schulze *et al.* (1998), about 33% of the complete value program was assigned to use value. Five full sample and five predicted sample values were taken from the complete clean-up, containment, public treatment, 10% shortfall, and 70% shortfall scenarios. An eleven-point estimate was derived from the disembedded use values.

Meta analysis variables

Building on the conceptual framework, the variables used in this analysis are grouped into core economic variables and study design effects. Unfortunately, because some of the studies did not include information on the level of variables included in their analyses, the variables selected for the meta analysis can only be loosely aligned with the conceptual framework. The core economic variables are suggested by the general conceptual model of option price for water quality discussed in Chapter 1 of this book. The study design effects capture information features of the studies and the type of question format.

Selection of study design effect variables was based on examination of within-study hypothesis testing and the criterion that these design effects had to appear in a minimum of three studies. This minimum studies requirement precluded some obvious variables raised in individual studies, e.g. phone versus mail (Crutchfield *et al.*, 1997). Such exclusion subjects the analyses to possible relevant excluded variable biases. While such biases may exist, the binary nature of these variables in combination with other binary covariates creates very unstable coefficients in the limited number of observations used here. Because of this result, a proliferation of additional explanatory variables would undermine the stability and replicability of our results.

Mean willingness-to-pay values reported in the individual studies were adjusted to 1997 dollars using the annual consumer price index. As indicated in Tables 8.1 and 8.2, there is a wide range in values both within and across studies. The following description of the explanatory variables used in the meta analysis is organized by variable group.

CORE ECONOMIC VARIABLES

The core variables used in all regressions in the analyses define the program by the type of change that will occur, the price vector of water including substitute sources, and the income level. Summaries of these variables by study are provided in Table 8.1.

The first variable in this core, D(USE), pertains to whether the program focused on use values associated with drinking water protection, or broad environmental and non-use values associated with aquifer protection. Non-use motives for ground water protection have been demonstrated generally for ground water (Mitchell and Carson, 1989) and shown empirically to exert a substantial influence on willingness to pay for ground water protection (Edwards, 1988; McClelland *et al.*, 1992). On this basis we would expect those studies that concentrated on filtration devices (e.g. Caudill, 1992; Jordan and Elnagheeb, 1993; Crutchfield *et al.*, 1997) or containment strategies (e.g., McClelland *et al.*, 1992) to demonstrate lower values than studies which value more broadly defined ground water protection programs. Such divergence in values is demonstrated within the McClelland *et al.* (1992) report. Letting D(USE)=1 if the study limited its focus to use values and zero otherwise, our expectation for the sign of this coefficient would be negative.

General quality change studies, as defined above, are used as the base for this analysis. Specific quality change studies are incorporated into the analysis with a binary variable D(ΔPROB) to measure whether specifying or eliciting contamination probabilities results in a general shift in values. This binary variable is multiplied by the contamination probability difference to create the variable ΔPROB. By default, general quality change studies are assigned a

Table 8.1. Core variable means for data used in meta analysis by study, organized by study type

	Survey [Survey Year]	OBS	WTP ($) 1997	D(USE)	D(ΔPROB)	ΔPROB	D(ΔSUPPLY)	ΔSUPPLY	D($SUBS)	I (thouands)
	Edwards [1986]	4	1,316	0.00	1.00	0.63	0.00	0.00	0.00	104
Specific Quality Change	Sun [1989]	23	1,126	0.00	1.00	0.59	0.00	0.00	0.00	55
	Jordan & Elnagheeb [1991]	4	126	1.00	1.00	1.00	0.00	0.00	0.00	30
	Poe Stage I [1991]	2	380	0.00	1.00	0.49	0/00	0.00	0.50	44
	Poe Stage II [1991-92]	10	324	0.00	1.00	0.50	0.00	0.00	1.00	47
	Crutchfield et al. [1994]	8	691	1.00	1.00	1.00	0.00	0.00	0.00	52
ΔSupply	McClelland et al. [1991]	11	117	0.82	0.00	0.00	1.00	0.40	1.00	51

	Survey [Survey Year]	OBS	WTP ($) 1997	D(USE)	D(ΔPROB)	ΔPROB	D(ΔSUPPLY)	ΔSUPPLY	D($SUBS)	I (thouands)
	Schultz [1988]	2	114	0.00	0.00	0.00	0.00	0.00	0.00	50
	Powell [1989]	12	83	0.00	0.00	0.00	0.00	0.00	0/00	44
General Quality Change	Caudill [1990]	6	64	0.33	0.00	0.00	0.00	0.00	0.00	53
	Delavan [1996]	5	59	0.00	0.00	0.00	0.00	0.00	0.00	47
	Bergstrom [1997]	9	199	0.00	0.00	0.00	0.00	0.00	0.00	46
	Boyle [1997]	9	46	0.00	0.00	0.00	0.00	0.00	0.00	33
	All Studies (weighted)		357	0.24	0.46	0.32	0.08	0.03	0.19	50

Table 8.2. Survey and elicitation effect means used in meta analysis by study, organized by study type

	Survey [Survey Year]	OBS	WTP ($1997)	D(CANC)	D(LOCAL)	PUBLIC %	D(PCARD)	D(DC)	D (DC- CAM)	D(DC-UTIL)	D(OEaft DC)
Specific Quality Change	Edwards [1986]	4	1,316	0.00	1.00	0.89	0.00	1.00	0.00	1.00	0.00
	Sun [1989]	23	1,126	0.50	1.00	0.87	0.00	0.83	0.13	0.70	0.17
	Jordan & Elnagheeb [1991]	4	126	0.00	0.00	0.50	1.00	0.00	0.00	0.00	0.00
	Poe Stage I [1991]	2	380	0.50	1.00	0.00	0.00	1.00	0.00	0.00	0.00
	Poe Stage II [1991-92]	10	324	1.00	1.00	0.00	0.00	1.00	0.50	0.00	0.00
	Crutchfield et al. [1994]	8	691	0.00	0.00	0.70	0.00	1.00	0.00	0.00	0.00
ΔSUPPLY	McClelland et al. [1991]	11	117	1.00	0.00	0.83	1.00	0.00	0.00	0.00	0.00

Survey [Survey Year]		OBS	WTP ($1997)	D(CANC)	D(LOCAL)	PUBLIC %	D(PCARD)	D(DC)	D (DC- CAM)	D(DC-UTIL)	D(OEaft DC)
	Schultz [1988]	2	114	0.00	1.00	0.90	0.00	1.00	0.50	0.00	0.00
General Quality Change	Powell [1989]	12	83	0.00	0.00	0.84	1.00	0.00	0.00	0.00	0.00
	Caudill [1990]	6	64	0.00	0.00	0.59	0.00	0.00	0.00	0.00	1.00
	Delavan [1996]	5	59	1.00	1.00	0.32	0.00	0.20	0.20	0.00	0.40
	Bergstrom [1997]	9	199	1.00	1.00	0.76	0.00	0.89	0.44	0.44	0.11
	Boyle [1997]	9	46	1.00	1.00	0.35	0.00	0.89	0.44	0.44	0.11
	All Studies (weighted)	105	357	0.46	0.62	0.58	0.23	0.60	0.17	0.20	0.14

D(ΔPROB) value of zero. A similar set of variables are created to isolate the quantity or supply studies, consisting of a binary variable D(ΔSUPPLY) and a change in supply variable (ΔSUPPLY). We formulate no expectation on the coefficients of each of these binary variables. However, coefficients on ΔPROB and ΔSUPPLY are expected to be positive based on the within-study results for the specific quality change studies (e.g., Edwards (1988), Sun *et al.* (1992), and Poe and Bishop, Chapter 3, this book) and the McClelland *et al.* (1992) research.

Two final core economic variables are included: the price of substitutes and income. The price of substitutes is included in the analysis as a binary variable, D($SUBS), to capture the notion that willingness to pay for water quality improvement is bounded from above by the opportunity for substitution through the establishment of a choke price. Hence we would expect the coefficient on this binary variable to be negative. Income, I, represents the final core variable, with values from individual studies updated to 1997 dollars using the consumer price index. Based on the theoretical construct and empirical findings in each of the studies that included income as an explanatory variable, we expect the coefficient on income to be positive.

While the conceptual model also specifies the own price of water before and after intervention, such information is not provided in any of the studies used. As such, we do not include a proxy for own price. Also excluded from the analysis is a simple variable indicating whether substitutes (e.g. filtration. bottled water etc.) were mentioned in the survey. Such a variable was not significant in the 1994 analysis, and almost all studies (with the exception of Shultz (1989) and Caudill (1992)) include a brief question or discussion of such opportunities. Another difficulty in trying to create a generic substitution variable is that there is quite a range of ways in which the substitutes are introduced across studies. In some cases discussion of substitutes is achieved through specific questions. For example, the Delavan (1997) survey asked 'In the past 5 years have you undertaken any of the following to improve the safety of your drinking water' with response options including 'installed a pollution protection devise,' 'installed a new well,' 'boiled your tap water' and 'bought bottled water.' Other studies (e.g. Poe Stage II) have augmented this question-based approach with information directly addressing the availability and cost of substitutes.

Study Design Effects

Four variables were used to control for variations in design effects across studies. The average of these variables by group are detailed in Table 8.2. Discussions with the authors of each study indicate that one of the central debates was whether or not to mention cancer, especially in the nitrate studies. The nature of this debate is characterized in Crutchfield *et al.*(1997, p. 6): 'To avoid alarming respondents or inducing so-called panic responses to the CVM questions, the discussion of the potential risks avoided the uses of trigger words such as 'cancer.' Instead we told respondents that 'nitrates are chemical substances hazardous to human health if taken in large quantities.'' Within study comparisons suggest that information bundles that contain mention of cancer do appear to elevate willingness-to-pay values (e.g., Bergstrom and Dorfman, 1994; Poe and Bishop, 1992). Also, one of the four regressions in our 1994 study indicated that the coefficient for those studies that mentioned cancer was positive. In the three remaining regressions the coefficient was insignificant. On this basis we would expect a positive coefficient on the binary variable D(CANC).

A second design variable, a binary variable indicating whether the locality was emphasized, D(LOCAL), is also expected to exert a positive influence on willingness to pay. This expectation draws from the experimental economics literature that suggests that group identification tends to increase cooperation (Ledyard, 1995). Thus, a study which focuses on or emphasizes a local county (e.g. Bergstrom *et al.*, Chapter 2 this book), town (e.g., Shultz, 1989) or community (e.g., Edwards, 1988) might have higher values than those studies that were conducted at statewide (e.g., Caudill, 1992) or national (e.g., McClelland *et al.*, 1992) levels.

The proportion of respondents connected to public water supplies may be regarded as an explicit design feature or simply an outcome of using broad mailing lists. Regardless, some authors have conjectured that this respondent characteristic exerts an influence on willingness to pay. Vandenberg *et al.* (Chapter 6, this book) suggest that private and public well users aren't valuing the same commodity in the sense that private well owners do not pay water bills, are not protected by drinking water standards, and may have a more intimate knowledge of their water supply. Hence, we would expect the willingness-to-pay function to be different across households with public and private sources of water. Jordan and Elnagheeb (1993, pp. 242-43) argue 'The private well users were willing to pay more than the city/county water users. An explanation for this result is the city county/water users are presently paying the water companies for water, while the private well water users are not. Another possible explanation might be ... the subjective expectations of the reliability of public versus private cleanup activities.' In contrast, Caudill (1992) found that rural households tend to be more confident that the quality of their water was safe, suggesting that they might have lower willingness to pay for general programs. Based on these mixed arguments, as well as the insignificance of this variable in the 1994 analysis, no sign expectation is reached for the variable PUBLIC % (i.e., the percent of the respondents connected to municipal supplies).

Two other design features were included in the 1994 meta analysis, but are dropped here. These are the response rate (as a proxy for study quality) and whether a specific contaminant was mentioned. Response rate is not included here because the link between this measure and the quality of the survey is highly conjectural and has not been demonstrated in previous meta analyses (e.g. Boyle *et al.* 1994; Loomis and White, 1996). Specific mention of the type of contamination is excluded because such mention tends to be highly correlated with the specific information approaches in this data set (the exceptions being the Maine and Georgia studies reported in Chapter 2 of this book and the Pennsylvania study reported in Chapter 4).

A wide body of experimental economics and contingent valuation research has demonstrated that estimated willingness-to-pay values are affected by how the question is asked. In particular, as noted by Randall *et al.* in Chapter 5 of this book, dichotomous choice typically generates higher values as compared to open-ended or payment card elicitation methods. To accommodate such effects we have incorporated binary variables to indicate whether the contingent values were collected using open-ended techniques (the baseline), payment card (D(PCARD)), or dichotomous choice (D(DC)) methods. Lacking a body of prior experiments, no expectation is formed concerning the coefficient on D(PCARD) variable. However, the coefficient on D(DC) is expected to be positive. A binary variable for open-ended values following a dichotomous choice question D(OEaftDC) was also included, based on the use of this design feature by Sun (1990), and Delavan (1997). Following the Epp and Delavan (Chapter 4, this book) and Randall *et al.* (Chapter 5, this book) findings that willingness to pay is positively correlated with the preceding dichotomous choice bid value, the coefficient on this variable is expected to be positive.

We have also incorporated two binary variables to indicate how the dichotomous choice willingness-to-pay value was calculated. Using the *ad hoc* willingness to pay estimated by the Hanemann (1984) approach as a base, separate binary variables were used to identify whether willingness to pay was estimated by the Cameron (1988) approach and/or whether a utility theoretic approach was used. Since the Cameron measure accounts for negative willingness-to-pay values while the Hanemann measure, as we define it, is restricted to non-negative values, the expected coefficient on D(DC-CAM) is negative. Based on the findings in Bergstrom *et al.* (Chapter 2, this book) we expect a positive coefficient on D(DC-UTIL).

META ANALYSIS RESULTS

In Table 8.3, we report three equations estimated by weighted least squares with standard errors derived using the Huber-White consistent covariance estimator. As noted in Smith and Osborne (1996, p. 293-94), 'this approach treats each study as the equivalent of a sample cluster with the potential for heteroskedasticity (i.e., differences in error variances across clusters).' The weights were created such that each separate study as depicted in Tables 8.1

and 8.2 were given equal weight, and with the weights of the individual observations within a study summing to one.

Each of the three models contain the core variables as discussed above. The first equation consists of only the core variables. The second and third models contain the core variables along with the study design effects. The 'Full' model uses all the variables indicated in the previous discussion. The 'Short' model retains all the core variables, but sequentially removes the least significant coefficients outside the core until all remaining coefficients obtained a pretest significance level of 20 percent or better. Consistent with the notion that we are looking for directional effects and consistency, discussion of these models focuses on the direction and the significance of the coefficients.

All of the coefficients in the core model are significant and of the expected sign, with the exception of the binary variable for specific quality change studies $(D(\Delta PROB))$, the binary variable for the change in supply studies $(D(\Delta SUPPLY))$, and the binary variable indicating that respondents were informed of the costs of substitute water sources $(D(\$SUBS))$. Importantly, the results in the core model are generally maintained in the more complete models. As indicated by the negative coefficient on $D(USE)$, studies that focused only on use values had significantly lower willingness to pay than studies that elicited total willingness to pay for complete clean-up. The change in probability variable, $\Delta PROB$, had a statistically significant coefficient with the expected positive sign. The high significance of the $\Delta PROB$ variable is likely to reflect within study variation as well as across study variation in the changes in probability. As noted, the coefficient on $D(\Delta SUPPLY)$ was not significant, suggesting that this approach does not systematically raise or lower values compared to the base general information model. The high significance on the $\Delta SUPPLY$ coefficient reflects the fact that these observations were drawn from only one study, and that the reported values were highly linear across rationing levels. Income level (I) is also a highly significant explanatory variable. The coefficient on $D(\$SUBS)$ is negative but not significant.

In the complete models, the cancer variable $D(CANC)$ has a coefficient with a positive sign that is statistically significant only at the minimum 10% level. This low significance level may be due to the fact that many of the surveys that mention cancer do so in a way that is intended to show that cancer is not a problem with the specific contaminant. For example, the Bergstrom *et al.* (Chapter 2, this book) questionnaire notes that 'Another health concern some people may have is whether or not nitrate in ground water is a risk concern for adults. After reviewing available studies, the US Environmental Protection Agency is *not* convinced at this time that nitrates in drinking water represent a potential risk of cancer'. The coefficient on the $D(LOCAL)$ variable is not significant, and is dropped in the short model. The percentage of respondents on public supplies is positive and significant at the 10% level in the long model.

Table 8.3. Estimated meta analyses for ground water WTP functions[a]

Variable	Type of variable	Expected Sign	Core Economic	Full Complete	Short Complete
Constant			-437.8871 (122.8006)[b]	-491.1078 (121.8075)[b]	-606.1551 (114.2564)[b]
D(USE)	Binary	-	-525.3888 (244.1817)[c]	-440.3059 (240.8310)[d]	-378.9782 (175.1660)[c]
D(Δ PROB)	Binary	?	-150.7279 (233.1261)	-174.1401 (228.7353)	-214.1035 (220.7103)
Δ PROB	Continuous	+	1116.1780 (357.6387)[b]	1085.1610 (348.6740)[b]	1106.0240 (348.0058)[b]
D(Δ SUPPLY)	Binary	?	401.4944 (342.3272)	235.4335 (221.0381)	206.1893 (192.1265)
Δ SUPPLY	Continuous	+	289.1667 (0.0000)[bc]	289.1667 (0.0000)[bc]	289.1667 (0.0000)[bc]
D($ SUBS)	Binary	-	-164.9097 (193.641)	-83.0452 (128.9884)	-55.7698 (102.5404)
I (thous.)	Continuous	+	12.3259 (2.4500)[b]	8.4125 (2.1409)[b]	8.5054 (2.2663)[b]

	Type	Expected sign	(1)	(2)	(3)
D(CANC)	Binary	+		186.8805 (111.6271)[d]	153.8043 (90.0627)[d]
D(LOCAL)	Binary	+		-121.1955 (146.8399)	
PUBLIC %	Continuous	?		210.4727 (121.8724)[d]	212.3484 (128.0199)
D(OEaftDC)	Binary	+		73.8525 (52.2359)	133.9757 (87.3535)
D(PCARD)	Binary	?		-93.5884 (86.8525)	
D(DC)	Binary	+		185.2280 (50.1987)[b]	214.1465 (79.5873)[b]
D(DC-CAM)	Binary	-		-181.0027 (25.7664)[b]	-192.8408 (33.0719)[b]
D(DC-UTIL)	Binary	?		227.4003 (101.3476)[c]	220.0108 (97.8578)[c]
n			105	105	105
R^2			0.74	0.83	0.82

Notes

[a] Numbers in () are asymptotic standard errors. The small standard error on the coefficient for Δs is due to the new linearity of the limit number of WTP observations in this sample.

[b] significant at 1% level.
[c] significant at 5% level.
[d] significant at 10% level.

The elicitation effects variables are universally consistent with prior expectations and the broader literature in contingent valuation. The coefficient on the payment card binary variable D(PCARD) tends to be negative, but never approaches standard significance levels. This is consistent with prior research suggesting that the open-ended and payment card approaches provide proximate values. Similarly, the D(OEaftDC) is positive, but not significant at standard levels. In contrast, the D(DC) and D(DC-CAM) coefficients are statistically significant and positive and negative, respectively. Again this corresponds with prior expectations. The D(DC-UTIL) coefficient is positive and significant. Such a finding is consistent with the conclusions reached in Bergstrom *et al.*(Chapter 2, this book).

It should also be noted that the additional explanatory variables in the complete models do appear to moderate the responsiveness of willingness to pay to some of the core economic variables, raising concern of relevant excluded variable bias. Notably responsiveness to the income variable appears to decline with additional variables.

IMPLICATION AND CONCLUSIONS

Our conclusions from this research closely reflect our earlier findings, even with the addition of a substantial number of data over the intervening years. In spite of wide variations in reported willingness-to-pay values reported in individual studies and a divergence of approaches to address the valuation of ground water quality, the meta analysis indicates that there is a strong systematic element of these studies such that we feel comfortable in concluding that as a whole, the emerging literature on ground water valuation appears to be demonstrating systematic variation.

Importantly, the core variables indicate that values do respond to whether total or use values are elicited, the magnitude of the change in probability of exceeding standards in those studies using that framework, and income. Echoing the findings of McClelland *et al.* (1992) willingness to pay was found to vary directly with the level of shortfall when a rationing program was indicated. Taken together, the high individual significance of these coefficients and the relatively high explanatory value of the core model (as indicated by R^2 values above 70 percent) suggest that willingness-to-pay values are systematically varying with components of the theoretical construct.

The direction of elicitation effects both reflects and should inform the broader CV literature. While the coefficients on the payment card and the dichotomous choice variables demonstrate what is already well established in the literature, the positive coefficient on the utility theoretic derivation of willingness to pay should be regarded as a new contribution, lending support to the within-study findings presented in Bergstrom *et al.* (Chapter 2, this book).

In contrast, study design variables other than the bid elicitation method did not appear to exert a robust influence on estimated ground water quality values as evidenced by the instability of these variables across model specifications. In part this may be due to the fact that coding these variables involved much more subjective criteria than the core bid elicitation variables. The D(CANC) binary variable, for example, is simply coded as one if cancer is mentioned in the questionnaire, even if the attempt of the survey was to downplay the risk of cancer. Likewise, all studies indicated locality to a certain degree, and the decision to code one study to emphasize locality while another study does not requires subjective judgement on our part.

Another plausible explanation for this apparent relative invariance in other design effects is that our present sample is inadequate for isolating such effects because we are drawing from a diverse set of studies with divergent methodologies. This latter interpretation suggests a research agenda in the future that creates greater homogeneity and power by conducting parallel studies that broadly remain within the spectrum of designs used in the current studies but focus on isolating the impacts of design effects. In short, we argue that extending the parallel studies philosophy represented in Bergstrom *et al.* (Chapter 2, this book) to design effects will allow researchers to better understand the factors that affect ground water values, thereby enhancing the policy relevance of this entire body of literature.

Given our finding that values across studies do vary systematically, it is natural to ask, 'Can the results of our empirical analysis be used as a benefits transfer function?' Perhaps they could, but we are personally extremely cautious about using meta analysis output to provide value estimates for policy decisions. Our viewpoint stems, in part, from concerns raised by Delavan and Epp in Chapter 7 of this book, that the amalgamation of a number of studies and theoretical constructs may lead to misleading magnitudes of coefficients. Given the disparity in research approaches adopted in the studies used in our analysis and our limited data set, such a concern is pertinent.

NOTES

1. Edwards (1988) also varied the time to contamination, the probability of demand, and the cost of bottled water. The latter aspect is not included in his 1988 paper, and is not apparent from the questionnaire copies provided from the author.
2. The Delavan (1997) study described previously closely followed this survey design. A critical difference from the perspective of this meta analysis is that Delavan specified a change in the probability of exceeding the contamination threshold.

REFERENCES

Bergstrom, J. C., and J. H. Dorfman (1994), 'Commodity information and willingness-to-pay for groundwater quality protection,' *Review of Agricultural Economics*, **16**:391-404.

Boyle, K. J. (1994), *A Comparison of Contingent Valuation Studies of Groundwater Protection*, Staff Paper REP 456, Department of Resource Economics and Policy, University of Maine - Orono.

Boyle, K. J., G. L. Poe, and J. C. Bergstrom (1994), 'What do we know about groundwater values? Preliminary implications from a meta analysis of contingent-valuation studies,' *American Journal of Agricultural Economics*, **76**(5):1055-61.

Cameron, T. A. (1988), 'A new paradigm for valuing non-market goods using referendum data: maximum likelihood estimation by censored logistic regression,' *Journal of Environmental Economics and Management*, **15**, 355-79.

Caudill, J. D. (1992), 'The valuation of groundwater pollution: the differential impacts of prevention and remediation,' Ph.D. Dissertation, Department of Agricultural Economics, Michigan State University.

Crutchfield, S. R., J. C. Cooper, and Daniel Hellerstein (1997), 'Benefits of safer drinking water: the value of nitrate reduction,' Agricultural Economic Report Number 752, United States Department of Agriculture, Washington DC.

Delavan, W. A. (1997), 'Valuing the benefits of projecting groundwater from nitrate contamination in Southeastern Pennsylvania,' Master of Science Thesis, Department of Agricultural Economics and Rural Sociology, Pennsylvania State University, University Park.

Edwards, S. F. (1988), 'Option prices for groundwater protection,' *Journal of Environmental Economics and Management*, **15**: 475-487.

Glass, G.V. (1976), 'Primary, secondary, and meta-analysis of research,' *Educational Researcher*, **5**(10):3-8.

Hanemann, W. M. (1984), 'Welfare evaluation in contingent valuation experiments with discrete responses,' *American Journal of Agricultural Economics*, **66**(2):332-41.

Hanley, N.D. (1989), 'Problems in valuing environmental improvements resulting from agricultural policy changes: the case of nitrate pollution,' *Discussion Paper in Economics 89/1*, University of Stirling.

Jordan, J. L., and A. H. Elnagheeb (1993), 'Willingness to pay for improvements in drinking water quality,' *Water Resources Research*, **29**: 237-45.

Ledyard, J.O. (1995), 'Public goods: a survey of experimental research,' in Kagel, J.H. and Roth, A.E. (eds), *Handbook of Experimental Economics*, Princeton: Princeton University Press, pp. 111-94.

Loomis, J. B. and D. S. White (1996), 'Economic benefits of rare and endangered species: summary and meta analysis,' *Ecological Economics,* **18**(3):197-206.

McClelland, G. H., W. D. Schulze, J. K. Lazo, D. W. Waldman, J. K. Doyle, S. R. Elliott, and J. R. Irwin (1992), 'Methods for measuring non-use values: a contingent valuation study of groundwater cleanup,' Draft Report, USEPA Cooperative Agreement #CR-815183.

Mitchell, R. C., and R. T. Carson (1989), Existence values for groundwater protection. Draft Final Report Prepared Under Cooperative Agreement CR814041-01. Washington, D.C. US Environmental Protection Agency.

Poe, G. L. (1998), 'Valuation of groundwater quality using a contingent valuation - damage function approach,' *Water Resources Research,* **34**(12): 3627-33.

Poe, G. L. and R. C. Bishop (1992), 'Measuring the benefits of groundwater protection from agricultural contamination: results from a two-stage contingent valuation study,' *Agricultural Economics Staff Paper Series No. 341,* University of Wisconsin-Madison.

Poe, G. L. and R. C. Bishop (1999), 'Valuing the incremental benefits of groundwater protection when exposure levels are known,' *Environmental and Resource Economics,* **13**(3): 347-73.

Poe, G. L., H. M. van Es, T. P VandenBerg, and R. C. Bishop (1998), 'Do households update their health risk and exposure perceptions with water testing?,' *Journal of Soil and Water Conservation,* **53**(4):320-25.

Powell, J. R. (1991), 'The value of groundwater protection: measurement and willingness-to-pay information and its utilization by local government decision-makers,' Ph. D. Dissertation, Department of Natural Resources, Cornell University.

Powell, J. R., D. J. Allee, and C. McClintok (1994), 'Groundwater protection benefits and local community planning: impact of contingent valuation information,' *American Journal of Agricultural Economics,* **76**:1068-75.

Schultz, S. D. (1989), 'Willingness to pay for groundwater protection in Dover, NH: a contingent valuation approach,' Master of Science Thesis, Department of Resource Economics, University of New Hampshire.

Schultz, S. D., and B. E. Lindsay (1990), 'The willingness to pay for groundwater protection,' *Water Resources Research,* **26**(9): 1869-75.

Schulze, W. D., G. H. McClelland, J. K. Lazo, and R. D. Rowe (1998), 'Embedding and calibration in measuring non-use values,' *Resource and Energy Economics,* **20**(2): 163-78.

Smith, V.K. and L. Osborne (1996), 'Do contingent valuation estimates pass a scope test? A meta analysis,' *Journal of Environmental Economics and Management,* **31**(3):287-301.

Sparco, J. (1995), 'A conjoint analysis of willingness to pay for changes in groundwater quality,' Selected Paper, Annual Meeting of the Northeastern Agricultural and Resource Economics Association, Burlington VT, June

1995.   Abstract in *Agricultural and Resource Economics Review*, **24**(2):258.

Stenger, A., and M. Willinger (1998), 'Preservation value for groundwater quality in a large aquifer: a contingent-valuation study of the alsatian aquifer, *Journal of Environmental Management*, **53**(2), 177-93.

Stevens, T. H. , C. Barrett, and C. E. Willis (1997), 'Conjoint analysis of groundwater protection programs,' *Agricultural and Resource Economics Review*, **27**(2):229-36.

Sun, H.   (1990), 'An economic analysis of ground water pollution by agricultural chemicals,' unpublished thesis, University of Georgia, Athens.

Sun, H., J. C. Bergstrom, and J. H. Dorfman (1992), 'Estimating the benefits of groundwater contamination control,' *Southern Journal of Agricultural Economics*, **24**(2):63-71.

van den Berg, J. C. J. M., K. J. Button, P. Nijkamp, and G. C. Pepping (1997), *Meta-Analysis in Environmental Economics*, Kluwer Academic Publishers, Dordrecht.

9. Summary and Conclusions

Kevin J. Boyle, John C. Bergstrom and Gregory L. Poe

INTRODUCTION

In closing this book we would like to summarize some of the key insights that arise from Chapters 2 to 8. Unlike journal articles on the valuation of water that focus on methodological issues where precise conclusions are drawn from statistical tests, it seems more appropriate to close with a synthesis that draws together key points regarding the valuation of ground water. While the focus of this book has been on ground water valuation, the insights we discuss also apply to contingent valuation studies of surface waters as sources of potable water. In our review of the literature, we found relatively few studies dealing with valuation of potable water quality outside of the ground water valuation studies mentioned in the chapters of this book (see Chapter 8 for citations). A number of previous studies have addressed the value of water quality in surface water bodies for boating, fishing, swimming and other forms of recreation (see Chapter 1 for citations). In addition, as mentioned in Chapter 1, studies have been conducted of provision of potable water by municipalities, but these studies typically assumed that municipal water supplies met federal and state potable water quality standards. Thus, while potable water is critical for human sustenance, the benefits of programs to protect or improve water quality have received very little attention.

The key areas of insight in this book that help to address this paucity of economic information deal with the development of original estimates of ground water values (Chapters 2, 3, 4 and 5), the conduct of benefit transfers when it is not possible to estimate original values (Chapters 6 and 7), and meta analyses of existing ground water valuation estimates (Chapter 8). Each of these topic areas also have implications for using ground water valuation estimates in policy analyses.

USING CONTINGENT VALUATION TO ESTIMATE VALUES FOR PROTECTION OR REMEDIATION OF POTABLE WATER

Several important insights arise from the applications in Chapters 2 to 5. The first is that the primary policy issues that require valuation estimates often involve maintaining ground water as an uncontaminated supply of potable water. Thus, the change in quality that is often valued is the change in the probability that the ground water is contaminated. Remediation reduces the probability of consuming contaminated ground water and proactive policies protect ground water from becoming contaminated.

Given this valuation focus, Bergstrom *et al.*, in Chapter 2, demonstrate that respondents' subjective perceptions of the change in the probability of contamination, with and without a protection or remediation program, constitute an important variable in analyzing responses to valuation questions. This result is confirmed in Chapter 4 by Epp and Delavan. In Chapter 3, Poe and Bishop demonstrate that the credibility of ground water value estimates can be enhanced by providing water users with specific information about contamination levels in the water source for a particular household. Thus, objective information on the probability of contamination is important in valuation scenario design, and respondents' subjective perceptions of the change in the probability of contamination are important for analyzing valuation responses.

Including objective data on actual contamination levels for individual households provides a real anchor in the valuation exercise. However, most policies will not be directed at individual wells or households. The policies will reduce the probability of contamination for all households in the area affected by the policy change. In addition, even with objective data on the probability of contamination, most respondents are likely to answer valuation questions based on their subjective perceptions of the reduction in the probability of contamination.

In designing a contingent valuation study of water quality, we suggest that respondents be given data on the *ex ante* (pre-change) and *ex post* (post change) probabilities of contamination, and subjective *ex ante* and *ex post* probabilities be elicited. Varying the change in objective probabilities, particularly the *ex post*, provides a mechanism for developing value estimates for a variety of changes in the probability of contamination. That is, at the time a valuation study is conducted, water managers may not know the exact change in the probability of contamination, but may have an idea of the range of the reduction. Having value estimates for a range of reductions in the probability of contamination allows customized value estimates for the actual reduction a policy is designed to accomplish or the reduction that is actually realized from implementing a policy. Using subjective probabilities can also allow for this flexibility, but the study design must allow for the subjective perceptions of the reduction to be linked to the actual reduction. Developing this link can be difficult and was not done in either Chapter 2 or Chapter 4. Using the damage function approach discussed in Chapter 3 may help to establish linkages between water quality values and actual changes in water quality parameters.

A final insight arises from the study by Randall, DeZoysa and Yu reported in Chapter 5. These investigators valued ground water as part of a policy package with surface water. This valuation framework makes conceptual sense given the physical interrelationship between ground water and surface water. Contaminated surface water can percolate into ground water supplies and percolating surface water can carry contaminants in soil into the ground water. In addition, ground water recharges surface waters. Thus, it is likely that any program to protect surface waters is likely to protect ground water and the converse also holds. Thus, valuing ground water and surface water concurrently makes sense from both a physical perspective and from a policy perspective. The difficulty, however, if that the physical dynamics of the interactions of ground water and surface water is often not well enough known to support this type of study design without making some very strong assumptions. To ignore this interrelationship is also a strong assumption.

BENEFITS TRANSFERS FOR VALUATION OF POTABLE WATER

The discussion of benefits transfer by Delavan and Epp in Chapter 7 presents a rather bleak picture of the possibility of conducting credible benefits transfer of ground water values, while VandenBerg, Poe and Powell in Chapter 6 present a more optimistic perspective. Further inspection of these two benefit-transfer tests clarifies these differing conclusions.

Delavan and Epp conducted their transfer using the Georgia and Maine studies reported in Chapter 2 and the Pennsylvania study reported in Chapter 4. Valuation surveys were administered within a single agricultural county in each state. The Georgia and Maine studies were identical, except for customizing comparable contamination information to local conditions. The Pennsylvania study contained some fundamental differences in how the contamination information was presented to respondents and how the valuation question was framed. VandenBerg, Poe and Powell (Chapter 6), in contrast, used results from a study where the same survey instrument was used in three states (Massachusetts, New York and Pennsylvania). The survey was administered in five communities in each state.

Thus, Delavan and Epp (Chapter 7) could only make comparisons across states and one state had a different survey instrument. They were not able to establish credible benefits transfer, even between Georgia and Maine where identical survey instruments were used. VandenBerg, Poe and Powell (Chapter 6) could make comparisons within and between states with an identical survey instrument; they found that credible transfers could be conducted within each state, but not between states. Thus, results in Chapters 6 and 7 are actually consistent in that benefits transfer appear not to work well when undertaken between states.

The question for future benefits transfer for policy analyses is to understand why the benefits transfer worked better within states but not between states. The design of the study reported in Chapter 6 does not appear to provide the intuition needed to answer this question. Thus, the results in this book suggest that there is hope for using benefits transfer when original value estimates for ground water are not available, but more basic research on this topic is needed before widespread use of benefits transfer is undertaken.

While we argue that the general insights regarding the design of ground water valuation studies apply equally to the valuation of surface waters, the same can not be said about benefit transfers. As suggested by the benefits transfer tests reported in this book, valuing similar commodities is an important condition for valid benefits transfers. Further benefits transfer tests are needed to determine if transferring values from a ground water commodity to a surface water commodity is credible.

META ANALYSIS OF POTABLE WATER VALUES

The meta analysis by Poe, Boyle and Bergstrom (Chapter 8) of ground water values presents a number of interesting insights for design of ground water and surface water studies. First, there is a very small library of ground water valuation studies. Second, inconsistencies in the designs of the studies and the study applications prevent including all of the existing studies in the meta analysis. Third, the results of the meta analysis lend credibility to the existing studies in that the variables in the meta equation, by their significance and signs, suggest that respondents to contingent valuation studies of ground water are responding in a manner that is logically consistent with economic theory. Finally, although we are personally cautious about using meta analysis results for benefits transfer, these results do perhaps provide some useful insight into how study site values may need to be adjusted before transferring value estimates to a new policy site. For example, while the probability of contamination may be fixed in any given study, it may vary across studies.

This variation across studies allows a statistical examination to be made of the effects of contamination probabilities as was done in the meta analysis reported in Chapter 8 (this book). Using the results of statistical analysis as illustrated in Chapters 6 and 7 (this book), it may then be possible to adjust water values across sites to account for differences in contamination probabilities at specific policy sites.

WHERE DO WE GO FROM HERE?

The chapters and discussion in this book suggest three primary areas of future research that can be applied to valuation of ground water, surface water and integrated ground and surface water supplies. First, the validity of water valuation estimates needs to be investigated. Are value estimates unbiased estimates of what people would actually pay? This is a crucial topic that has received scant attention in most valuation studies of potable water.

Second, there is a need for more water valuation studies, especially with respect to potable water supplies . There have been very few valuation studies of ground water and there is no depth in any single geographical region and no depth in the type of contaminants outside of nitrate contamination. Even fewer studies exist of the economic value of the quality of potable water obtained from surface water supplies. There are no studies that we know of that value water quality from a systems perspective explicitly recognizing and modeling the hydrological and ecological linkages and interrelationships between ground and surface water supplies.

In the water policy and management arenas, there is often interest in and debate related to using secondary data sources for valuing water quality protection and remediation. A necessary precursor to developing more credible benefits transfer is a need for more original studies and more work on the validity of original estimates. This recommendation also applies to developing value estimates for protection or remediation of potable surface water supplies.

Third, more research is needed on when credible benefits transfer will work as acceptable proxies for an original study. Among other questions, why did VandenBerg, Poe and Powell in Chapter 6 find credible transfers within states but not between states? Is there some commonality of preferences within states? Is it due to differing institutional structures of ground water protection within states? Is it due to common types of contamination within states, but not between states? The extent to which estimates of the economic values of water obtained from ground water supplies can be transferred to surface water supplies and vice versa is another benefits transfer area where more research is needed.

In closing, we hope that this book has helped to highlight key features of theory, practice and application of valuation of potable water for public policy. We hope that the book also helps to synthesize water valuation insights from the existing literature, in addition to documenting available secondary sources of water quality valuation data. Finally, since there are still many unanswered questions related to the economic valuation of water quality, we hope that this book will prompt further research on the valuation of the protection and remediation of potable water supplies.

REFERENCES

Boyle, K. J. and J. C. Bergstrom (1992), 'Benefits transfer studies: myths, pragmatism, and idealism,' *Water Resources Research*, **28** (3): 657-63.

Index

Accidental spills 2, 144

Aesthetic benefits 7

Aggregation 97, 116, 121

Aggregation effect 113-114, 117

Agricultural chemicals 144, 162

Agricultural crop irrigation 6

Anchoring 67, 79, 80-81, 131, 134

Anchoring effects 79

Aquatic ecosystems 6

Aquifer 1-2, 147, 162

Bacterial contamination 1

Benefit-cost analysis 3, 19, 100, 117, 122, 134

Benefit function 102-104, 107, 112-117, 135-6

Benefits transfer 13, 56, 100-102, 104-106, 108, 110, 112-119, 121-23, 125, 128-9, 131-6, 165-7

Bid elicitation method 159

Blue baby syndrome 42-3, 53, 69, 145

Boatable waters 2

Bootstrap 53, 55, 58

Cancer 42-3, 69, 145, 152-153, 155, 159

Censoring 36, 73, 78, 81, 94-5, 125

Changes in production costs 7

Chemical contamination 1, 5

Chlorination 75

Climate 6, 121

Commercial
 fishing 6
 hunting/trapping 6, 8
 plant gathering 6

Complex policy package 83

Conditional mean 131

Conjoint analysis 7, 16, 140, 161-2

Contingent valuation method 7, 12, 14-16, 21, 36-7, 50, 55, 64, 77, 81-3, 89, 98, 101, 104, 119, 123, 136-7, 139, 143, 154, 158, 160-164, 166

Convergent validity 77, 102-103

Convolutions technique 55

Cost-benefit analysis *see* benefit-cost
  analysis

Damage function 16, 39, 56, 58-9, 63-4,
  161, 165

Damages avoided 7

Defensive expenditures 7, 13

Dichotomous-choice 21, 50-52, 57-8,
  64, 67, 71, 98, 124, 126, 131, 145

Direct transfers 112-117

Drinking water 1-2, 5-7, 9, 11-12, 15, 23,
  37, 42-6, 67, 69, 73-5, 77, 80, 103,
  105, 109, 119, 141-2, 144, 146-7,
  152-3, 155, 160

DWEABS method 84

Economic services 3,5-6

Ecosystem 2,6

Elicitation format 73, 77-9, 81-2

Embedding questions 146

Endangered species 65, 123, 136, 161

Erosion control 6

Experimental economics 63, 153-4

Expert opinios 101

Farm livestock wastes 74

Fertilizer applied to farms 74

Fishable waters 2

Flood control 6

Food product processing 6

Functional
  equality 115
  form 83, 93-6
  inequality 115
  transfer 123-5, 133

Gamma distribution 95-6

Garbage dumps 74

General quality change 139, 143, 147

Geothermal power plants 6

Golf courses 2, 74

Ground water 1-3, 5-6, 8, 12-13, 19-22,
  38, 46, 50, 55-6, 58-9, 64, 76, 80,
  82-3, 103-104, 139, 140-141, 143-
  5, 155, 163-7
  contamination 6, 19, 21, 23, 38, 77,
    104-105, 109, 126-7
  protection 12, 20-21, 24-6, 28, 30,
    32, 34, 37, 39-41, 51, 55, 76-7, 79-
    80, 104, 109, 113, 118, 125-7, 137,
    139, 143-7, 167
  quality 12,13,18-21, 35-6, 66, 100-
    102, 104, 117, 121-5, 127, 134,
    137, 139, 145, 158-9
  safety 77, 105, 123-4, 126

Grouping effects 113-114, 117

Hedonic price method 7

Information 3, 9, 12-13, 21, 36-46, 48-
  50, 52-6, 59-60, 62-5, 67-9, 75-6,
  80, 93, 102-103, 105, 117, 119,
  121, 124-5, 134-5, 139-143, 145-6,
  152-4, 160-161, 163-5
  bias 68
  overload 55

Informational imbalance 53, 55

Informed open-ended 70, 74, 81

Interstate transfers 115

Intrasite error 125

Intrinsic services 6

Item non-response 58, 87, 105

Landfill 74, 144, 146

Livestock consumption 6

Log-normal distributions 95

Logistic function 53, 71

Manufactured goods production 6

Market scope 121

Meta analysis 13, 36, 118, 137-144, 146-7, 154, 158-162, 166, 167

Multi-component programs 89, 93, 97

Multivariate probit analyses 90, 97

Municipal supplies 79, 97, 146, 153, 163

Naive transfer 133

Natural resource damage assessment 3, 63, 136

Nitrate 11, 16-17, 21-2, 36, 38-51, 53, 55-60, 62, 64, 66-9, 75, 79-80, 82-3, 119, 121-2, 124-5, 140-145, 152-3, 155, 160, 167

NOAA panel 97-98

Non-use
motivations 40-41, 63
value 8, 15, 37, 64, 80-81, 119, 147, 161

Off-site nature observation 6

Objective probabilities 23, 140, 164

OLS model 95, 125

On-site nature observation 6

Open-ended questions 19, 23, 67-8, 77-8, 81, 124-5, 130, 134

Option price 8, 10,14, 18-21, 23-6, 28, 30, 32, 34-6, 38-9, 41, 82, 102, 118, 139-141, 146,160

Parametric bootstrap 53

Passive use
services 6, 8
values 84

Payment card format 105, 118, 124, 141, 144, 146, 154, 158

Policy site 101-3, 106-7, 112, 114, 116, 123, 166-7

Polychotomous choice 81

Potable water 5, 6, 8, 163-8

Potential Pareto-improvement criterion 88

Prior water testing 45, 52, 55

Private
home septic systems 74
lawns and gardens 74
well 9, 21, 41, 43, 66, 73, 77-80, 105, 126-7, 141-5, 153

Probit choice function 87

Prospect reference theory 40

Protest
bidders 19, 23-5, 35-6, 80
responses 71-2

Public
water supplies 9, 42, 66, 73, 75, 77, 106, 145, 153

well 43, 141-2

Quality   1-3, 5-12, 19-21, 23, 35-9, 55-6, 59, 64, 66-8, 70, 74, 88, 100-104, 107, 109-110, 117-9, 123, 135-7, 139-141, 147, 152-5, 158-165, 167-8

Quantity 1,2,7, 139, 145, 152

Random utility 124, 136

Recreational
  boating 6
  fishing 6-7, 123
  hunting/trapping 6
  plant gathering 6
  swimming 6

Referendum 36, 63-4, 71, 81, 83-4, 87, 93, 95-6, 99, 160

Remediation 9,10,12, 19, 160, 164, 167-8

Research method effects 19

Response function 48, 51, 53, 70-71

Risk
  assessment variable 19, 23-4, 35
  perceptions 16, 18, 38, 41, 44-5, 49-50, 59, 64-5, 70, 111, 119, 142

Safe drinking water 2, 145

Safety
  difference approach 145
  questions 49-50

Septic tanks 20, 42, 144

Sewage plants 74

Soil erosion 14, 83

Specific quality change 139-140, 143, 147, 152, 155

Split sample design 97, 141

Starting point bias 79, 81, 93, 98

Stated preference methods 7-8

Study
  design effects 139, 146, 152, 155
  site 106-107, 112-113, 116-117, 123, 166

Subjective
  probability 9, 20, 23, 58-60, 62, 140
  risk perceptions 18, 70
  utility 40

Substitutes 59, 139, 152

Surplus preservation model 93-4, 96

Surface water 1-2, 5-6, 12-13, 83, 98, 135, 163, 165-7

Swimmable waters 2

Tobit regression 77-8, 131

Toxic chemicals 144

Transformation function 40

Travel cost method 7,16

Trichlorethylene 104

Truncation point 63, 72

Uncertainty 3, 8, 11, 39, 45-6, 48-50, 54-5, 64, 75, 80, 82, 123

Underground storage tanks 144

Unit-day use values 101

Use value 146-7, 155, 158

Utility theoretic approach 24, 154

Valuation function 63, 102

Value
elicitation procedure 19
of life hypothesis 59

Verbal protocol 70, 75

Visibility 64, 123, 139

Voting
behavior 88
response 87-88

Waste disposal services 6

Water
market demand functions 7
quality commodity 3
quality monitoring 3, 5, 21
quality services 3, 5
rationing 146

Well protection 144

Wetland
ecosystems 6
habitat 83

Willingness to pay 7-8,10-11,13-16, 23,
37, 40, 56, 66, 70-72, 75, 77, 99,
101, 109, 119, 123-6, 130-131, 139-
140, 142-4, 146-7, 152-5, 158, 160-
161